The Little Book of Carla Connor

A decade in the life of a soap queen

An Unofficial
Coronation Street Companion Book

By Glenda Young

First published in May 2016 by Glenda Young

Cover design by Jo Blakeley

Dedication

This book is dedicated to all Coronation Street fans,
everywhere in the world,
from up north to down under
and everywhere else in between

Alison King's awards for playing the role of Carla Connor (as at Friday May 27 2016)

2007
TV Times Awards
Sexiest Female

2008
Inside Soap Awards
Best Bitch

2008
TV Times Awards
Sexiest Female

2008
Daily Star Soaper Star Awards
Best Bitch

2009
TV Times Awards
Sexiest Female

2010
Inside Soap Awards
Best Stunt - Factory Siege

2012
British Soap Awards
Best Actress

2014
RTS North West Awards
Best Performance in a Continuing Drama

2015
Inside Soap Awards
Best Actress

2015
TV Choice Awards
Best Soap Actress

Facts and Figures about...
Coronation Street's Carla Connor

Date of birth
January 3, 1975

Father:
Johnny Connor

Mother:
Sharon Donovan

Husbands:
Paul Connor
Tony Gordon
Peter Barlow
Nick Tilsley

Siblings:
Rob Donovan (half brother)
Kate Connor (half sister)
Aidan Connor (half brother)

First appearance:
December 1, 2006

Final appearance:
May 26, 2016

Played by:
Alison King

Carla Connor makes an entrance

It's Christmas time in Weatherfield and there's a festive mood on Coronation Street. However, the knicker factory Christmas party is strangely subdued. It's fair to say that the mood is rather sombre at the Underworld Christmas party the year that brothers Paul and Liam Connor take charge.

As the girls and Sean moan the lack of a Christmas party, a stranger storms into the factory. Knowing full well how to make an entrance, the woman strides into the factory, holding a bottle of champagne high in each hand. She surveys the sorry scene in front of her.
'Looks like I'm in the very nick then! Ker-flamin'-ching! Enter Chrimbo drinks fairy!'

The factory girls turn to stare at the glamorous newcomer. All eyes are on her as she explains who she is.
'Carla. I expect Paul's told you all about me?'
'My lovely wife,' Paul announces to his stunned workforce.
Later, Paul tells Carla he hopes that she'll make an effort to become friendly with the factory girls.
'Do I look like I've got ugly mates?' she replies. As Liam and Paul get to grips with running the factory, Carla decides she wants a piece of the action too. She has dreams of designing her own range of kids clothes but Paul doesn't want her anywhere near his factory.

He and Carla have a marriage built on mistrust and dislike. And so, when Carla tells Paul she wants to start her own business, Paul's very much against it. Liam isn't keen either.

Determined to get her own way, Carla cosies up to Kelly Crabtree at the factory and offers her some work on the side to get her new kids collection underway. Carla knows how unpopular her side venture will make her with her husband and brother-in-law, but still she carries on with her plans. Managing to make herself even more unpopular, she buys a desk and moves it into the Underworld office.

Liam persuades Paul to have a quiet word with his missus about her kids clothing project. But Paul's too scared to say no to his wife, and so Liam does it for him. When Liam tells Carla she can't use the factory girls to do her work, she comes up with a plan to use the factory after hours, instead.

Offering slave wages to Becky Granger, Joanne Jackson and Kelly, the girls take the work as they're desperate for cash. Becky even brings in another girl from the homeless hostel to help with the stitching. The girls take on as much overtime from Carla as they can get.

Liam takes a shine to Joanne and the two of them share a secret snog on the factory floor. Liam wants their fling kept a secret but Joanne blurts it out to the factory girls to stop Kelly from carping on about how much Liam fancies her, when he clearly doesn't.

But it backfires on them all when Carla sacks Joanne. She says that if Joanne's thick enough to fall for Liam then she's not safe to work a sewing machine.

There's good news for Carla when she gets an order for her kids clothes from Trendy Tots. But she can't afford to pay her workers even the minimum wage to get her kids clothes stitched. Sally Webster, Fiz Brown, Hayley Cropper and Joanne meet in the Rovers for a good moan. They're afraid that if the Connors can get away with paying less than the minimum wage to Carla's clothes stitchers then they'll end up doing the same to them too.

One of the workers Carla has been paying is a Polish girl, Kasia. She works all the hours the Connors can squeeze out of her on both the day-shift and the night-shift. Tired and overcome with exhaustion, after working through the night, Kasia loses her footing as she walks down the Underworld steps. She's got her arms full of boxes and can't reach out to steady herself. She falls heavily and lands badly at the bottom of the stairs and tumbles to her death. Kasia's death isn't covered by the Connors' insurance as she died on what was officially the nightshift. And so Carla and Paul decide to keep quiet until after 8am when they ring an ambulance and pretend she was working on the day shift.

It's around this time that Carla notices Paul acting very oddly. As well as hitting Michelle's son Ryan, Paul drives off with a car full of samples they were supposed to show to a buyer. The buyer leaves Underworld empty handed and less than impressed. Liam reveals to Carla that Paul is distraught because memories have been flooding back to him about what really happened to Ryan's dad, Dean.

He tells Carla that he had been out one night with Paul and Dean in Dean's car. Dean was driving and they'd all had too much to drink. Dean was so drunk that 'he was trying to put his car key in the stereo,' says Liam. That's when Paul insisted on driving instead but on a deserted stretch of road Paul lost control of the car. Dean was killed instantly. Liam and Paul made the decision to drag Dean's body and place it behind the steering wheel so Dean would take the blame for the crash and Paul would keep his license. They made a pact not to tell Dean's wife Michelle. But now the truth is out and Carla knows just how devious her husband can be.

She also finds out how nasty Liam can be when he tells her that he wants her out of the factory. Liam has Carla's desk shifted and removes all her stuff. When she complains, he just mocks her: 'Shouldn't you be out skinning dogs for a new coat?' Carla takes herself to the pub and unleashes her bad mood on the nearest Connor she can find - who just happens to be poor Michelle. When Michelle defends her two brothers, Carla lets slip that she wouldn't be so kind about them if she knew the dark family secret they'd been keeping from her for years.

Paul Connor

'You!' says Paul when he finds out who the escort girl is who's turned up at his hotel bedroom.

'You!' says Leanne Battersby when she finds out who the escort agency has sent her to meet.

Instead of getting down to business, they sit and have a drink in Paul's hotel room. When Paul returns home the next day, Carla finds him in the Rovers. She wants to know where he's been all night.

'I'm under no illusions, Paul,' Carla tells him. 'I know that wasn't the last night I'm going to spend on my own wondering whether you're dead or alive.'

'I'll try to make more of an effort,' Paul says, not too convincingly. 'I promise.'

Just then, Leanne walks into the Rovers. Without knowing what's gone on the night before between Leanne and Paul, Carla's relieved to see someone else at the bar.

'Oh, at last, somebody sane,' she says to Leanne. 'Come and join us, quickly, before I die of marriage.'

But Paul has trouble keeping quiet about Leanne. When he finds out that Liam has been seeing Leanne he warns his brother to stay away from her.

Still unaware that Leanne's working as a prostitute, Carla takes Leanne out for lunch to the pizza place in the precinct. As the ladies lunch, Carla comes up with a mad idea for her and Leanne to go into business together and buy the pizza place. Leanne stalls for time, she doesn't have the cash or the business sense.

But this doesn't stop Carla railroading Leanne into agreeing to become her business partner. Paul is incensed when he finds out that Carla wants to spend their cash to buy the pizza place. And when he finds out Leanne plans to be Carla's business partner, steam just about comes out of his ears. To find the cash for her share, Leanne has to go back on the game to earn enough money in a very short time.

Leanne and Carla agree to go ahead with the restaurant deal. They crack open a bottle of bubbly, drink to independence and decide to name the restaurant Valandro's. Carla says she'll never sully herself by working at Valandro's and leaves the running of the place to Leanne. However, the two of them soon have a major falling-out. It's not long before Carla's calling Leanne 'a dirty little tart' after Carla's propositioned by a man in a bar who assumes she's on the game, like Leanne. There's clearly more to Leanne than Carla knows about.

And she soon finds out what Paul has been up to with escort girls when she checks his credit card statements. She notices he's been paying over the odds for 'Secretarial Services' and checks up on the payments, discovering Paul's guilty secret. With nothing to lose, Paul comes clean about crossing paths with prostitutes, including Leanne.

'Paul. You have been caught with your trousers round your ankles and your credit card on the bedside table!' cries Carla. 'Do you seriously think you can persuade me this is just another daft adventure in our rollercoaster of a marriage?'

'Like I said once before when faced with a tricky question - I do,' Paul replies. 'These girls. They don't mean anything. I could pass any one of them in the street and I wouldn't recognise them.'
'Except Leanne,' Carla says.
'I never slept with Leanne.'
'Really? That's what she says too. At least you got your story straight.'

Paul storms out of the house, angry and desperate to find Leanne to get her to tell the truth to Carla. First, he rings the escort agency, asks for Leanne and they meet at a hotel.
'Beg Carla to take me back,' Paul tells Leanne. 'She thinks we slept together.'

Paul and Leanne leave the hotel and walk towards Paul's car. He uses the remote control to release the lock on the boot.
'Come here I want to show you something,' he says.
Leanne follows Paul to the back of his car.
'What?'
'This!'
Paul grabs Leanne and bundles her into the boot of the car. She struggles but Paul is too strong.
'Sorry love but do you think I'd let you ride in the front of my car?'
'What're you doing? Paul! Get off!'
'Come on. There's a good girl. Mind hands!'
Paul slams the boot shut. Leanne screams and bangs on the inside of the boot.
'Change of plan, Leanne. You wrecked my relationship so I'm gonna wreck yours. Make yourself comfortable, it could be a bumpy ride.'

Once inside the car Paul rings Liam.
'Meet me at the flat. I've got something to show you,'
then he presses his foot to the floor and the car races
off. Inside the boot, terrified Leanne manages to get
her phone out of her bag to call her mam Janice.
Liam calls Paul back, desperate to know what's going
on. Paul is driving erratically and his phone has
fallen into the passenger side footwell. When his
phone rings, he reaches across and leans forward to
retrieve it but the phone is just out of reach. As he
looks up at the road, there's panic on Paul's face. In
that split second, he loses control of the car as it races
towards a junction. The last thing that Paul Connor
sees is a moving lorry as it crashes into him at full
speed. In the boot of the car, Leanne is seriously hurt,
but alive.

While all of this is going on, Carla's in the back room
of the pub getting very, very drunk with Michelle.
'You don't like me do you?' she asks Michelle.
Michelle's too polite to say 'no' even though Steve
has already starting calling Carla 'Cruella DeVorce'.
'I never said I didn't like you,' replies Michelle.
'True, that was me. But I was right though, wasn't I?
See I don't get it. All I ever wanted was to be part of
the gang but you wouldn't let me in. I wasn't good
enough.' Carla downs her wine, laughing.
'That's a laugh, innit? Me... not good enough for
your Paul. A dead slug is too good for your Paul.'
'What did he do to you?' asks Michelle.
'We're the same you and me. We loved him and he
lied to us both.'

'Are you going to tell me what he's done?'

Carla pours more wine for herself. 'Where do I start?'

'Well, try the beginning 'cos I've got a feeling it's going to be a long night.'

Steve comes into the back room and interrupts their conversation. He tells Carla and Michelle that he's just had a phone call from Liam saying there's been an accident involving Paul.

'What kind of accident?' Michelle cries, alarmed.

'Nothing trivial, I hope,' says Carla.

At the hospital, Liam, Michelle, Steve and Carla are there along with Janice who is waiting for news on Leanne. The nurse warns the Connors to prepare for the worst possible news about Paul.

Liam is aghast when he sees the state of Carla at the hospital.

'Are you drunk?' he demands to know.

'Not as drunk as I'd like to be,' she says. 'Is there a bar in here? The Doctor's Arms? The Old Aneasthetist? The Scalpel and Stethoscope?'

Janice is having a hard time understanding what Leanne was doing in the boot of Paul's car. It's a question that everyone wants answered and it's Carla who reveals the dark truth.

'Your girlfriend Leanne is a prostitute,' she spits at Liam. 'And your big brother is her number one customer.'

As the shock news sinks in for everyone, Carla adds: 'See, told you we could have done with a bar!'

Paul's injuries in the car crash prove fatal and the Connors fly over to Ireland where his funeral is held. When they return home, Carla doesn't feel ready to head home alone to her flat and stays with Michelle for a while. She finds Leanne to tell her she's pulling out of the Valandro's deal, saying she'd rather go into business with the devil than into partnership with her.

Carla takes charge

After Paul's death, Carla struggles to cope at first with work and managing the factory. But it doesn't take long before she's firing on all cylinders, with Hayley's help. She continues to crack the whip at the factory and lets the girls know she's very much back in charge. Oh yes, Carla DeVille, as Janice now calls her, takes no prisoners and has the girls working overtime on Sundays. She promotes Hayley to line manager and gives her a pay rise. And it's in that thrusting frame of mind that Carla greets Liam when he returns to work. She tells him that Underworld belongs to her now. She owns the majority share since Paul's death.

'I'm the boss, get used to it,' she tells Liam. 'You're working for me now.'

Carla hires Rosie Webster as her admin assistant. This knocks Sally's seams out of kilter when she finds out that her daughter's working with management while she's still on the shop floor. Acting as Carla Connor's mini-me, Rosie Webster throws herself into the bear pit of stitching and bitching at Underworld while making the tea and keeping Carla sweet.

Carla then sacks Joanne, saying she was last in, first out. She reckons it's a good enough reason to sack Joanne, the factory girl whom Liam likes best. Liam reinstates Joanne but she's sacked again by Carla. Joanne threatens to sue for unfair dismissal.

She also threatens to sue Liam for sexual harassment. But Carla knows how Joanne's mind works. She offers her a cheque to pay her off and make her leave quietly. It's a cheque that Joanne quickly accepts.

Liam's not happy taking orders from his sister-in-law at work. But in the months following Paul's death, Liam and Carla slowly become drawn to each other. At first, they try to deny their feelings, but once they're working so closely together at Underworld - temptation is with them all day. Liam desires Carla a lot, too much. He knows she isn't right for him but that doesn't stop him lusting after his sister-in-law.

Determined to stop Carla from getting under his skin, Liam starts dating Maria Sutherland. He rushes into proposing to Maria, despite his own misgivings and Carla's jealous warnings. As Liam grows close to Maria, Carla becomes jealous especially when she finds out that Maria's pregnant with Liam's baby. But as the pregnancy news filters around the street, Maria's doubts about Liam begin to creep in. She becomes unsettled when she finds out that Liam and Carla once shared a snog. Liam tries to sooth Maria's worries about Carla and takes her away on holiday to the Lake District. They don their funky new waterproofs and head off to the peaks with Ozzy the dog. However, they don't bother to check the weather forecast and miss the storm warning. While they're out fell walking, the weather takes a turn for the worse and Liam falls, ending up badly hurt.

The Mountain Rescue Team abseil down the mountain and stretcher Liam away to hospital in a helicopter. But at the hospital, there are words that Maria doesn't want to hear. The nurse tells her that Liam's waking words were a heartfelt plea for '…his Carla.' Making a speedy recovery, Liam limps back to the cobbles on crutches. Maria doesn't want Carla to know that Liam's back in town and she lies to her about where he is. Maria heads into town, shopping for her wedding dress. Meanwhile, Carla's enjoying a spot of lunch with Tony 'my knight in shining Armani' Gordon and spies Maria through the window of a wedding frock shop. Carla storms inside and there's an altercation, the likes of which the Vincent Malone Bridal Boutique has never seen before. Maria does her best to warn Carla away from chasing after Liam.

'Stay away from me, you vile cow,' says Maria.
 'You'd best buckle up love,' Carla warns her. 'You're in for a bumpy ride.'

Carla pulls out all the stops when she finds out Liam's back on the street. She cooks him a bacon, sausage and cheeky cheese casserole, just like his Irish mammy used to make. Knowing that Carla is going after Liam, Maria worries whether she will be able to hang on to him. In an act of desperation she brings the wedding date forward. When Michelle finds out that Maria's changed the date, she gives her a few words of warning.

'If there are cracks in your relationship, you can't paper over them with confetti,' she says.

Liam Connor

Carla's nose is put right out of joint when the Connor clan reunite for Liam and Maria's wedding. Helen and Barry Connor, the parents of Liam and Michelle, fly in from Ireland for the wedding of their younger son Liam to Maria, while dishing out vitriol to Carla, the widow of their deceased son Paul. It's fair to say that there's no love lost between Helen and Carla.

Audrey Roberts offers to put Helen and Barry up at her place on Grasmere Drive and gets their room ready using her best duvet cover. As the Connors and Maria enjoy a drink in the Rovers, Helen regales them with a tale of how a daily half pint of stout did her no harm when she was pregnant. She says drinking the black stuff is the reason her kids all have glossy, black hair. Leaving the Rovers, Maria heads off for a sleepover at Audrey's on the night before the wedding. This leaves the coast clear for Carla to slip round to see Liam to try to talk him out of marrying Maria.

Over at Audrey's house, Maria realises she hasn't got something old, something new, something borrowed and something blue. Emily comes up trumps with the borrowed and the blue by offering Maria a blue scarab which her nephew, Spider, sent to her from abroad. Maria nips back to the street to secure the scarab from Emily's house and while she's there, she's shocked to see Carla kissing Liam in the street.

The day of Maria and Liam's wedding dawns and Maria's in tears. She phones Liam to say she can't go through with it because of Carla's plotting and kissing and texting and snogging. Audrey does her best with: 'Ooh, now, come on, Maria my love,' but Maria demands to speak to her groom before the wedding takes place.

Waiting for the ceremony to begin, the wedding guests fidget as they wait while Maria speaks to Liam. Steve checks his watch and Kelly picks her teeth. Sally says she knew something bad was going to happen because she'd seen a single magpie on the way to the church. And that's never a good sign.

While Maria's having her heart to heart with Liam, his phone beeps with a message. It's from Carla, begging him not to marry Maria when he can have her instead. Well, you can't blame Carla for trying, but Liam Barrington Connor makes his choice, and marries Maria Jane Sutherland instead.

Kirk does his bit and proudly walks his sister down the aisle after telling her he's 'in loco parentis', a new phrase that he's just learned from Roy Cropper. Carla is in tears and storms out, but Maria's not quite finished with Carla just yet. Furious, she hunts down Carla and finds her in the ladies.

'So, are you not going to congratulate me, then?' spits Maria.
There's a pause before Carla allows herself to say the word: 'Congratulations.'

Maria eyes up Carla. 'Even on his wedding day you couldn't leave him alone, could you?' She shakes her head at Carla. 'How sad is that?'

'He's my mate,' Carla says. 'And I didn't want him making the biggest mistake of his life.'

'Right, he's your mate is he? Is that why you just told him you wanted him?'

It's clear from the look on Carla's face that she's shocked to hear Liam told Maria about her text.

'Have you got nothing to say to that, Carla? That's not like you, is it? You've usually got loads to say for yourself.' Maria tries to mimic Carla, ' 'Me, right, I can have him any time I want'.. yeah, right.'

'Shut up you smug little cow. You got him in the end didn't you?'

'So can we draw a line underneath all this now, eh?' asks Maria. 'Are you going to back off, leave us alone?'

'I might do,' Carla whispers. 'I might not.'

Maria's heard enough and slaps Carla hard across the face. Carla just smiles back.

'Everything he said out there, that you're sweet, kindhearted. You really fooled him, didn't you, Maria?'

'Me and Liam got married today. We made a commitment to each other. Now, whatever you imagined you might have, just forget it. Move on, Carla. Have a bit of dignity for once in your life.'

Tony Gordon

Carla tries to distract herself after Liam marries Maria by concentrating on her new relationship with Tony Gordon. The two of them continue get on so well that Carla asks Tony to move in. He then surprises Carla by offering to buy Liam's share of Underworld. But does Tony really have designs on lingerie or does he want to control Carla?

When he gathers Carla's family to her flat for dinner and menaces *'Marry Me'* across the table to Carla, it wasn't a question, it was more of a command. Carla wavers until she sees the size of the ring and then she caves in to Tony's proposal. Later that night, Tony flies off on a business trip to China. Carla and Liam are left alone in the flat after pregnant Maria goes home early, tired out. The next morning, Liam still hasn't returned home. Maria's beside herself with worry wondering what went on between Liam and Carla. Nothing did, as Liam spent the night on Carla's sofa. But Maria's got worse things to worry about when she tells Marcus Dent, the midwife, that she hasn't felt her baby move for a while.

Marcus takes Maria to the maternity ward where a scan reveals the worst – Maria's baby has died. A stunned Maria goes back to the street looking for Liam but can't bring herself to tell him what's happened. He's been swearing undying love to his wife and child. Without the baby to keep them together Maria knows she will mean less to him, so she hides her grief for now.

Maria takes refuge in Audrey's house where Audrey gets the news about her stillborn baby out of Maria, sob by tearful, heart-rending sob. With Maria holed up at Audrey's out of Liam's reach, she knows that as soon as he finds out the devastating news, he'll have no reason to stay with her. And she fears that it'll be Carla who Liam will go to for support.

When Maria eventually breaks the news to Liam, he struggles to cope with the death of their baby. Maria distances herself from her husband, sure that there is something going on between him and Carla - and she is right. Maria packs her bags and moves in with Fiz. Now then, I'm not sure that moving in with Fiz is the best place for poor Maria. The girl's just gone and lost a baby, buried him in a funeral and split up with her husband who's having a fling with his sister-in-law. Does she really need comforting from someone who wears fluoro blue eye shadow, a permanent grin and gives glib advice: 'I bet he'll come bursting through that door any minute saying 'Maria, I want you back' and you'll wonder what all the fuss was about.'

Desperately wrestling with his emotions and in turmoil, Liam seeks comfort with the person who knows him best. Soaked to the skin after he walks to Carla's flat in the rain, Liam rings the buzzer to her flat. Carla's heart skips a beat as she opens the door to Liam. He's soaked through - and he's in a foul mood, blaming Carla for trying to break his relationship with Maria. Carla refuses to accept any blame and tells him: 'You're captain of your own ship, Liam!'

'You're walking round in your home-wrecking boots every day, right under my nose,' he tells her.

'My footwear's to blame for the breakdown of your marriage, is it?' Carla shouts.

'No, not just your shoes. Your clothes, your make-up, everything about you. Your hair…'

'My hair?' she yells, incredulous. 'Do you realise how ridiculous you sound?'

Liam walks towards her, pointing his finger at her face. 'And that mouth especially, the constant sniping and flirting and hinting… the damage you cause with that bright red smacker.'

Carla turns on him, outraged. 'My wardrobe is not responsible for your libido and neither is my lippy!'

'Standing there like you haven't been trying to lead me astray or… or put pressure on Maria. You tried to ruin my own wedding day by dragging me away from her!'

'Yeah!' screams Carla. 'And you know why I did that! You know what I was trying to avoid, do you, now?'

The two of them are just inches away from each other now.

'This!' Carla cries.

'I wouldn't be here if it wasn't for you,' Liam says. 'I'd be at home with Maria, where I belong.'

'Well it's a funny place to have come, then,' Carla whispers to him.

Liam shakes his head. 'You are the root cause of everything.'

'You fancy me like crazy,' Carla says. 'That's the root cause of everything.'

Liam turns and walks away from her, unable to handle the truth.

'If you didn't exist I'd be a happily married man.'
'Oh. So what shall I do then? Shall I just disappear into a puff of smoke? Would you like that? Would that solve everything? Or would you miss me? Would she really be enough for you?'
Their argument escalates and gets out of hand, resulting in Liam walking out. But he's not away for long. Carla lets him back into her flat and apologises to him.
'I'm sorry,' she says, hugging him. 'I'm sorry for everything you've been through,'

A song plays in Carla's flat as they hug, a song that they both know well. It's the song that they'd danced to together at Liam's 21st birthday when she was dating Paul.
'I can't believe you caught me listening to this,' she tells Liam.
'It's a nice touch,' he says.
'What a giveaway, eh?'
'My 21st,' he reminds her. 'You dragged me up to slow dance.'
Liam admits that he'd fancied Carla, even back then.
'I remember,' she says. 'I remember thinking if it doesn't work out with Paul then his brother's all right.'
'Well, there's a thing,' Liam says.
'What did you think of me back then? Honestly? What did you think of me the day you met me?' she asks.
'Like the first time Richard Burton saw Elizabeth Taylor,' he smiles. 'She looked so beautiful he almost laughed out loud.'

'You see… how come nobody ever says that about me?'

'I just did.'

'Liam... Come to bed with me,' Carla whispers.

'What do you think I'm here for?' he replies.

Finally, after years of waiting, lusting and hoping, Liam kisses Carla full on the lips.

The next morning, Liam kisses Carla goodbye outside of her flat. Unbeknown to them both, Rosie Webster is waiting for Carla outside of her flat and films their kiss on her phone. Carla reckons she knows what Rosie is up to and tries to buy her silence with a great big handbag. It keeps Rosie quiet, for now. But Carla will need more than handbags to keep the smile on her face after Liam tells her he is going back to his wife. With their cases packed and Ozzy the dog bundled into the back of the car, Liam and Maria set off on their holidays leaving Carla on the cobbles, alone. Meanwhile, the evidence of Carla and Liam's kiss remains inside Rosie's phone.

When Liam returns from holiday, Carla demands that he sells his factory share to Tony. She blackmails him by saying if he doesn't sell she will tell Maria about the steamy events that have gone on between them. Tony gives Liam a 'take it or leave it' low offer. Liam has no choice and signs his share over to Tony.

Liam's cousin Tom Kerrigan then turns up out of the blue. Tom's a man with money worries. His Lads Rags t-shirt business that he runs with Liam has been turned down for a bank loan.

Tom doesn't tell Liam the bad news about the loan, he goes straight to Carla instead and asks her to invest. Carla almost purrs. It's a gem of a deal, and one that Liam's all a-fluster about when Carla tells him about it. Carla doesn't want Tony to know about her new deal with Lads Rags. Likewise, Liam doesn't want Maria to know about Carla investing in the business either. And so there are lots of secret business meetings between Carla and Liam, forcing them together again.

Meanwhile, Tony upsets office assistant Rosie at work and Carla tells him to sort things out. Trying to make amends, Tony takes Rosie for a meal in a posh hotel called Baden House. Rosie ends up quite tipsy with all the wine they drink with dinner. At the end of the meal she gives Tony a surprise – it's a room key hidden inside her napkin. Inside the hotel room, Rosie strips to her undies and offers Tony a glass of champagne - and much more. She's embarrassed and angry when Tony turns her down, saying that Carla is the only woman that he wants. Incensed by his rejection, Rosie shows Tony the video of Carla kissing Liam. Tony has little choice but to believe her when faced with such evidence.

He pours coffee down her to try to sober her up, then he leaves, telling Rosie to find her own way home. Spying on Carla and Liam, it's not long before Tony catches the pair of them sharing another long passionate kiss outside Carla's flat.

Tony's furious now he knows what Carla and Liam are up to. But he stays quiet while his wedding plans to Carla go full steam ahead. Planning his next move carefully and slowly, Tony offers to take Carla, Liam and Maria away for a weekend. On their mini-break, the girls stay at the hotel for a spa experience while Tony drags Liam out sightseeing. He knows Liam's scared of heights and so Tony takes him inside of a deep, steep cave. Liam's holding on for dear life in a damp, wet cavern. With Liam terrified, Tony asks him to be his best man at his wedding to Carla. Liam can't think of anything he'd like less but has no choice other than to say yes.

Back home from the weekend away, Carla tries on her wedding frock in the flat. Liam's there to see it and overcome with desire, he seduces her while she's wearing it.

On Tony's stag night, all of Tony's mates turn up wearing tartan and Tony Gordon face masks. At the same time, Carla's hen night in the Rovers takes place. There's a male stripper in the pub who brings out some whipped cream and Liz McDonald sprays it all over his chest.
'Hey!' screams Deirdre Barlow. 'Ken likes that cream! We have it on our apple crumble!'

With the lads paintballing on the stag night, and Carla partying on her hen night, Liam starts texting his love to her. Carla runs to the ladies, in tears and confides the truth about her affair to Leanne.

She advises Carla to go after Liam, lay her heart on the line and tell him she wants him as much as he wants her.

Taking Leanne's advice, Carla decides to head off to find Liam … but on her way out of the Rovers, Maria announces she's pregnant with Liam's baby, again.

Carla stops dead in her tracks. She knows that if it comes to Liam having to make a choice between his child and her, she'd lose out. So she has a few tears and a cigarette outside of the pub where Deirdre joins her.
'I didn't know you smoked,' Deirdre says.
'It's been thirteen years since I had one.'
'Are you nervous?' Deirdre asks.
'Just sifting through old memories,' Carla replies.
'Well, I'll smoke to them!' laughs Deirdre.
Deirdre notices Carla looks upset and asks her if she's made the right decision to be wed. Carla starts crying.
'It's nothing that a bit of lippy won't sort out,' she says.
'Now there's a rule to live your life by!' notes Deirdre.

Meanwhile, on Tony's stag night, Liam realises he's lost his wallet. Tony suggests he go back to the last pub they were in to find it. Liam turns to walk back to the pub and that's when a car screams out of nowhere, heads straight for him and runs him down to the ground, dead.

The lads gather around Liam's body, all of them in shock. None of them had seen the car, it had come speeding out of nowhere. One minute Liam was laughing and enjoying himself, the next he was gone, lifeless, the victim of a cruel hit and run. Tony gently cradles Liam's head as an ambulance is called. Maria arrives, sobbing uncontrollably when she sees her husband lying on the road. As she holds her dead husband in her arms and whispers the news to him that she is pregnant again, Tony's evil eye twitched as he felt the slightest twinge of guilt. Later, down by the canal, Tony throws Liam's wallet into the murky depths. Then he gives his car-driving henchman a wad of used notes in payment for the murder of Liam.

Liam's parents Barry and Helen fly in from Ireland again, this time for Liam's funeral. Maria's parents also arrive from Cyprus and there's more tea and tears than they all know what to do with. Liam's wake is held at the Rovers where there are sandwiches and singing. After the wake, Maria's parents leave their distraught daughter on the street and dash back to their donkey sanctuary in Cyprus.

After the funeral, heartbroken Maria starts sorting through Liam's belongings, with tears in her eyes. Her suspicions about Liam and Carla deepen as she goes through his phone and uncovers messages and calls to and from Carla.

Meanwhile, over at the Webster house, Tony demands that Rosie keeps quiet about the film of Carla snogging Liam. When Sally finds out, she's suspicious about Tony's motives for keeping the snog secret. Sally copies the video to a memory stick, just in case.

Soon after Liam's death, Tony starts to feel the murky waters of debt puddle around his ankles. To tide him over the flood of his financial crisis, Tony moves funds from Underworld to his own business account. He even forges Carla's signature on the company cheque.

To help recover from the death of Liam, her soulmate and the love of her life, Carla heads to Los Angeles to stay with a friend. With Carla away, the Underworld girls are up in arms when they find out they haven't been paid. Tony knows the reason why there's no money in the Underworld account, but he keeps them sweet by throwing £10 on a table in the Rovers. He tells the girls the drinks are on him, knowing how easily they can be bought. And he's not wrong.

When Carla returns from Los Angeles, it's all systems go for her elaborate wedding to Tony. On her wedding day, Carla's in a purple wedding gown, Tony's in a kilt and there's a man on the bagpipes. When she walks up the aisle, Liam's cousin Tom whispers to Carla: 'You look gorgeous!'.
'I know,' she replies.
'You take my breath away,' Tony tells her when she reaches his side.
'Hiya to you an' all,' she smiles at her groom.

Carla says her vows to Tony: 'I join my life with yours. Wherever you go, I will go. Whatever you face, I will face.'

There's gossiping at the back. Sean leans in to Janice and says: 'I thought marriage was supposed to make you a nicer person, what do you reckon the chances are with these two?'

'Slim to none,' Janice replies.

Carla continues with her vows: 'Come riches or poverty, I take you as my husband and I will give myself to no other.'

'Bit late for that,' Kevin Webster laughs.

The registrar then announces: 'With the authority vested in me I now pronounce you husband and wife. You may kiss.'

Carla kisses her new husband as the bagpipe player strikes up and the guests give a round of applause.

At the reception, the wine flows and the Websters get very drunk indeed. Kevin is so drunk that he spills guacamole down Carla's wedding dress. The Websters are in such a state that Carla lets rip at Sally and tells her to behave herself or she'll throw her out. 'Sally, I realise your family don't usually come to places that use metal cutlery but do us a favour, will you? If you lot can't behave at least half-civilised, there's a pub over the road with a pool table. Maybe you'll feel more comfortable there, eh?'

Sally's embarrassed and turns to Rosie: 'How dare she talk about my family like that? If people knew half the things that dirty cow's been…'

'Mum, please …' says Rosie.

Sally decides to exact her revenge on Carla for humiliating her at the wedding. She shows Maria the video of Carla snogging Liam. Maria spends the rest of the week questioning everyone as to whether they knew anything about Liam and Carla's affair. She's beside herself with worry and grief and becomes a woman possessed with finding out the truth.

Carla and Tony head off on honeymoon. When they return, Tony calls to see Maria after he listens to her rants on his phone accusing him of murdering Liam. Maria has deduced that Tony killed Liam because he was jealous about Liam's fling with Carla. Tony doesn't deny any of Maria's claims and tries to blackmail her into keeping quiet. Maria becomes deranged and tries to warn everyone on the street about Tony but no-one takes her seriously. She even reports Liam's murder to the police while Tony sits in his car fingering a leather belt with thoughts of murdering Maria.

However, there is someone who believes Maria's claim that Tony killed Liam. Jed Stone has witnessed Tony meeting his henchman Jimmy Dockerson and he tells Maria he knows that she's right. Armed with evidence about Tony's evil deeds, Jed tries to blackmail Tony at Underworld. But Jed's no match for Tony who tries to kill Jed by strangling him with an Underworld negligee! He bundles unconscious Jed's body into a basket at the factory. But when Tony goes back the next day to dispose of Jed's body, it's gone!

Jed's still alive, but where has he gone? Emily knows something's up when she finds Jed's hat in her house - and Jed Stone never goes anywhere without his hat. Or indeed his cat, which Norris has found in a basket. The hunt for Jed Stone carries on as Maria's nervous breakdown continues.

Maria's determined to prove that Tony Gordon killed Liam and she daubs the word …

MU DERER

… on the Underworld wall. Becky does the decent thing and paints in the missing R.

Maria finally manages to put doubts into people's minds about Tony. She convinces many of the residents of the street into believing that Tony killed Jed. He's so worried by this that he drives to Jed's home town of Wigan to find him. Tony drives Jed back to Weatherfield and parades him around the Rovers to prove to everyone that Jed is alive and quite well. Tony's strange behaviour with Jed makes Carla suspicious too and a few days later she heads off to Wigan to have a word with Jed. She treats Jed to a long liquid lunch in the hope that he'll talk but Jed's scared to tell Carla that Tony tried to kill him. However, when she spots strangulation marks on Jed's neck, that's when she realises her worst fears about her new husband are true.

When Tony discovers what Carla has been up to in Wigan, he sends the factory girls home early and locks Carla inside Underworld. Distraught after Liam's death, Carla has secretly wondered if Tony knew about her affair with Liam and she'd been suspicious about his involvement in his death. Not one to beat about the bush, Carla confronts Tony in the factory. The two of them argue and Carla admits that she slept with Liam, even while she was planning her wedding to Tony. Tony calls it subterfuge.

'Oh we had subterfuge all right,' Carla spits at him. 'We even had subterfuge in my wedding dress!'

To Carla's horror, Tony says he's got a confession to make.

Carla spits in his face and he reels away from her, chuckling.

'Don't think I don't know what it's like to feel murderous, Tony!'

'If you think I'm a cold blooded killer, why aren't you scared of me?'

'Maybe I am,' she says. 'I know you were jealous of him.'

'Oh please.' laughs Tony.

'All right I'll say it. Me and Liam. It'll never be over. I'll always have feelings for him.'

'Even though he's dead?'

'Especially now he's dead. You've made me love him more.'

'I knew. I'm not daft. Or blind.'

'So you killed him. I loved him, Tony. I loved him more than I ever loved you. D'you wanna know why? Because he walked better than you, he talked better than you, he was better in bed than you.' Carla's words rattle Tony and he starts trembling as the confession spills from his lips.

'I can't lie any more,' he cries. 'I killed him… I had him killed.'

Carla kicks Tony, hard, between the legs and escapes from the factory. She drives off in the rain as Tony sinks to his knees, crying.

Luke Strong

Who are the Women of Wilmslow? It's a tough question but one that needs to be asked because they're getting their knickers in a twist. There's a big order going out of the factory to the Women of Wilmslow and the man who comes to inspect the seams at Underworld isn't best pleased. He sulks about the stitching and growls about the gussets. With Carla away in Los Angeles again, Tony tries to placate him and their argy-bargy acts out on the factory floor. As the two men argue, Luke Strong walks into Underworld and announces that he's the new factory boss!

Luke is a childhood friend of Carla's. While she's away in LA she's asked Luke to come into the factory to look after it for her. Tony follows this up with Carla's solicitor who confirms it's all true.

Yes, Luke Strong is a man on a mission, determined to make his presence felt at Underworld. Clad in black and driving a red sports car, Luke Strong is clearly not the sort of man who would ever take a bus. He buys the girls and Sean drinks in the pub and tells them things won't be any different while he's around. He says it'll still be: 'Routine, familiarity…',
'… and chips?' asks the girls.

However, Luke's reign at Underworld lasts only a few months.

When Carla phones to say she is returning to Weatherfield, Luke hatches a plan to disappear. He ends up cheating Rosie Webster out of over £150,000. The cash was her compensation from John Stape after he kidnapped her. But that means nothing to Luke, who steals her cash and heads off to Brazil.

With Carla back from LA, desperate Tony rings Jimmy Dockersen, his henchman, and takes out a contract to kill Carla. Jimmy goes to Carla's flat intending to murder her, but Carla gives Jimmy more than he bargained for. She thwarts his murderous attempts and fights back. She hits Jimmy hard, with a candlestick, just as Tony arrives. Tony sees the state of Jimmy and convinces Carla that she's killed him, even though Tony knows that Jimmy's still alive. He covers Jimmy with a blanket so that Carla can't see Jimmy's still breathing. Carla's in a state and Tony advises her to disappear to Los Angeles, which she does.

When Carla returns the factory girls seem glad to have her back.
'She might be a bitch, but she's our bitch,' coos Sean from behind his sewing machine. Carla tries to concentrate on work until news reaches her that Tony has turned himself into the police for Liam's murder.

She also finds out that while she'd been away in LA, Tony tried to kill Roy Cropper by pushing him into the canal. After Tony's confession to the police, he's finally sent to jail.

However, it doesn't take long for Michelle to find out that Carla knew all along that Tony killed her brother Liam. Michelle is horrified when she finds out. The two women meet at the court after Tony has been jailed for Liam's murder.

'So, are you going to tell us now, are you?' Michelle asks Carla.

Carla braces herself. 'Tell you what?'

'Did you know?' asks Michelle. 'That it was your husband that killed Liam? Is that why you went running off to Los Angeles or wherever it was?'

'How would I have known a thing like that?' Carla says, unnerved.

'Maybe you guessed? Or maybe he just came straight out and told you. I mean you were sharing his bed, surely you knew what he was capable of?'

'If I told you I didn't know, would you believe me?' Carla asks.

'Probably not, no.'

'Then I'd be wasting my breath wouldn't I?'

Carla makes a move to leave but Michelle stops her. 'Did you know?'

'No. No. I didn't know. And I've got better things to do than stand here being shouted out. Now you'll excuse me, won't you?'

Carla sweeps past Michelle and Ryan and walks away from them both.

'And what if she did know? What difference would it make?' asks Ryan.

'The difference it'd make is I'd know just how much to hate her,' spits Michelle.

After Tony is jailed, Carla's in need of support at the factory. She tells Hayley: 'I need you Hayley. I've really had the stuffing knocked out of me recently and I need someone here I can rely on, see, and that's you. You're not going to let me down, are you?'
'No,' Hayley says. 'Of course not, Mrs Gordon.'
'Connor,' Carla says. 'No more Gordon. Carla Connor… it feels right.'

Trevor the bin man

Trevor Dean, the local bin man, starts lodging with Janice. When he first meets Carla he mistakes her for the factory cleaner when he walks into Underworld. It's an easy mistake to make as Carla's wearing an overall and washing the floor. He tells Carla he's looking for Janice and as they chat, Trevor admits he's a bit nervous of bumping into the factory boss after everything Janice has told him about her.

'Oh yeah, why's that?' smirks Carla, wondering what Janice has been saying about her behind her back.

'Janice and Kelly were going on about her this morning,' he says.

'What did they say about her?'

'Says she's up her own backside, mutton dressed up as lamb, bit of a dragon, that kind of thing. I can't remember word for word. Why? Do you like her?'

'Oh I couldn't possibly comment,' says Carla. 'I mean I'm just a lowly cleaner after all.'

When Trevor bumps into Carla later in the Rovers, she's all dolled up and Trevor's taken aback at the sight of her.

'Hello again!' he says. 'Blimey, that minimum wage goes a long way. You're the smartest cleaner I've seen, best looking an' all.'

Trevor invites her out for a drink in the Rovers and Carla finally comes clean about not being the factory scrubber.

Meanwhile, Janice goes on a diet as she thinks Trevor might be more interested in her if she loses a few pounds. But while she's on the lime and soda instead of pints of beer and she's eating salad instead of pie, Trevor's eyeing up Carla who invites him on a date. Janice prepares supper ready for a night in with Trevor. But he's nowhere to be seen. He's in bed with Carla after she lures him back to her flat after a few drinks in town.

Factory siege

Tony Gordon breaks out of jail with the help of his former cellmate Robbie Sloane, who's just been released. And the first thing Tony does is to storm back to the street. He's got murder on his mind and puts a gun to Carla's head when he finds her inside Underworld. He tapes Carla's mouth shut and ties her to the executive swivel chair in the factory. And then he finds Hayley in the factory and ties her up too. With the two women taped up and tied down, Tony throws petrol around after shooting Robbie dead to the factory floor. Just then, Maria walks into the factory where Tony's intent on setting the place alight. Carla screams at her to get help and Maria runs out to raise the alarm.

Hayley manages to wriggle free from her chair. Tony throws her out of the factory and onto the cobbles as the cops buzz outside and a crowd gathers to find out what's going on. Inside the factory there's only Carla and Tony. Tony's got a gun in one hand and a glass of whisky in the other.
'So! Just you and me now, like it was before,' says Tony. 'This is how it ends.'
He drains his glass.
'There's some more whisky in the bottom drawer,' says Carla, trying to stall for time. 'Don't suppose you've got one for me, have you? There's some chocolate Hobnobs in the biscuit tin. Why don't you untie me and we can have a drink to celebrate saving Hayley's life?'
'I thought you were more of a red wine kind of a girl?'

'You remembered. We could go on Mr & Mrs.'
'Along with that Macbeth couple? And Eva and
Adolf?'
'No I think you have to be married.'
' Is this your plan?' Tony asks. 'Keep me talking?'
'You can talk all night if you want to.'
'Do you really think you're going to go to sleep
tonight and wake up again in the morning?' he
threatens.
'I'm the eternal optimist me, aren't I?'
'You're already dead!' he yells at her, making her cry
even more.
'Real tears! Who are those for?'
'Us,' she lies.
'You destroyed us!'
'I loved you!'
'You don't know the meaning of the word,' he spits.
'We could have been so happy.'
'I was happy!'
'Is it too late to say I'm sorry?' cries Carla. Tony
walks over to her and holds her head in his hands.
He's desperate to know why Carla dumped him for
Liam.
'Why did you do it?'
'I don't know. Maybe something's not wired up right
in my head. I don't know.' Carla screams, terrified.
'Maybe you and me are more alike than we want to
admit.'
'Look at what we've done. Look at the lives we've
wrecked. We don't deserve to live.'
'Why not?' she asks him. 'I thought we just … let's
get out of here, eh? We could go somewhere, just me
and you.'

'We're going to be together, forever.'

Carla's desperate now. 'What if we had a baby? What if you had one of your own, wouldn't it give you something to fight for? Something to live for, eh, Tony?'

'No babies!' he yells, then he lets Carla go and drops the gun to the floor. He kicks the gun away, flicks the lighter open and sets the petrol ablaze.

'It's time to say goodnight,' he yells into the fire. 'It's over!'

The factory goes up in flames and Carla struggles so hard to get out of the chair that she finally manages to free herself. She throws the chair at Tony and he falls over. He reaches out and grabs her ankle and Carla falls to the floor too where the two of them fight.

'You're going nowhere!' Tony yells at her. 'Look at the flames, don't fight it, don't fight it!'

Smoke starts to bellow from the factory out onto the street. Just then Trevor turns up, demanding to know where Carla is.

'Last thing we heard, she was tied to a chair and he had a gun,' says Julie Carp.

'Are you winding me up?' says Trevor.

'I wish we were,' replies Janice.

Inside the factory, there's smoke and flames everywhere. Carla runs and barges into Tony, takes his gun and fires at him. The shot hits him in the arm and as gunshot is heard outside on the street, armed police arrive. Carla keeps the gun in her hand, pointing at Tony.

'You won't do it,' he sneers at her. 'You don't have the killer instinct, in business or anywhere else!'

'Don't come any closer! I mean it. I'm warning you. There's no way I'm going to die by your hand,' Carla says. 'I'll fight you to my last breath!'

'I love it when you talk tough. Come on. Smash my face in. We can die fighting.'

'Come on them, have a go,' she yells at him.

'Oh feisty!' Tony yells back. 'That's why I fell in love with you!'

Carla runs and makes her escape from the factory. Outside there's a round of applause and cheers when they see Carla coming out. Trevor rushes to her side just as Tony walks out. Then Tony stops… and turns… and walks back into the inferno...

Phoenix rising from the ashes

After Tony's death and the factory siege, Trevor and Carla go away to South Africa on holiday, to watch the football World Cup. When they return, Carla surveys the burned down remains of the factory and decides to rebuild it.

She then discovers that Nick Tilsley has started a rival company to Underworld. It's called Nick's Knicks and he's running the business in a unit under the viaduct. When she finds out that Nick's not only started a rival company but has stolen her workforce, she swans round to see him and gives him hell. 'You're a puffed up little ponce!' she yells at him.

Then Carla does what any good businesswoman would do faced with a rival who's tried to rip her off. She undercuts Nick's bottom line in knickers and sets out to rip him off. Nick finally agrees to work alongside Carla and it's not long before she rules the roost in the makeshift factory under the viaduct. Meanwhile, the builders start work to rebuild Underworld. Carla gives the building work to Izzy's dad Owen Armstrong who starts the job quickly with a bunch of lads working hard. When Underworld is rebuilt and the factory workers move back in, Carla gives boyfriend Trevor a job there. He works a week's notice on the bins before he moves into his new role as Carla's office assistant. But Trevor's useless, he really is.

He can't type, he can't answer the phone, and when he rips through a package of silk, Carla's at her wits end. It gets worse when Trevor hits Nick at work after he calls him a moron.

This causes more bickering between Carla and Trevor. Trevor's had enough and walks out, leaving Carla to her new love affair with the bottle of whisky she keeps in the bottom draw of her desk.

Realising she might be starting with a drink problem, Carla plucks up the courage to attend an Alcoholics Anonymous meeting at the Rita Tushingham Community Centre. As she walks into the group, she bumps into Peter Barlow.
'Sorry, wrong class,' she lies, excusing herself, 'I was looking for Conversational Spanish.'

Carla's problems continue when Nick says he wants her to buy him out of the business. He needs his share of the knicker factory to invest in his new bar at the old Turner's Joinery. Nick's news knocks Carla sick and she starts drinking whisky again. Drunk, she slumps into her car as she tries to drive to town to see her bank manager. It's Peter who stops her from driving off and killing herself, or anyone else. He gives Carla his number to call and offers her his support.

Carla's in denial about having a drink problem but Peter knows the signs. He's been there, drunk that, fallen off that sofa, sent his flat up in flames and almost killed his son.

Each time Carla calls him for help, Peter responds. But he lies to Leanne about where he spends his time, saying he's been helping out a drunk mate called Carl.

Nick steps up his demand for his money from Carla for his share of the factory. She gives him £5,000 less than he asks for. Carla's no mug. But Nick is - and he takes the money and runs to his solicitor to get his hands on the deeds of his new bar which he names The Joinery. He gives the job of bar manager to Leanne. She fills the place up with fixtures, fittings and fit fellas when she gives Irishman Ciaran McCarthy a job as their chef. As The Joinery sallies forth towards opening night. Betty's not happy when she finds out that Ciaran's nicked her hotpot recipe and that he's serving it up, tapas style. In fact, so incensed is she that she rings the council and gets revenge by reporting rats in the kitchen at Nick's new bar.

With Nick and Leanne now working closely together in the new bar, Nick confesses his love for his ex. At the same time, Peter and Carla start to cosy up too. Michelle becomes suspicious of Carla after she finds out that she's been ringing Peter. When Michelle drops Carla off at her flat and spies Peter walking in, she asks if Carla and Peter are having an affair. Carla confesses all. Well, almost all. She confesses that she's been drinking and driving. She confesses about having been sentenced in court and losing her license. But she keeps quiet about how she's tried to seduce Peter wearing nothing but her bath towel and a welcoming smile.

However, there's a shock in store for Carla, and for all the residents of Coronation Street. Devastation and destruction rocks the street after a gas explosion at The Joinery destroys the viaduct, causing a tram to fall and crash into the Kabin. Peter was inside the Old Joinery at the time of the crash. As soon as the emergency services arrive, they bring out the bodies – some alive, some dead. Peter's rushed to hospital but it's not looking good. He can hardly breathe, never mind speak, but in the aftermath of the shock of the tram crash, he demands to marry Leanne right there and then in his hospital bed. A vicar's called and vows are exchanged before Peter's sped into the operating theatre.

As Leanne waits for news from the doctor in the hospital she's more than a little confused as to why Carla's so cut up about Peter too. She also starts wondering why Carla's hanging round the hospital. It slowly dawns on Leanne that Carla is 'Carl' the alcoholic whom Peter's been helping. The two women sling words at each other in the hospital foyer as Leanne tells Carla to stay away from her husband.
'He's got internal bleeding round the heart!' Leanne cries.
'Oh, haven't we all?' Carla snipes back.

It's touch and go for a long time for Peter but he finally pulls through. His first words are to his new wife, Leanne: 'Hiya, Mrs Barlow.'

Frank Foster

There's a new customer at Underworld who brings a firm jaw and well-turned suit to the street. But he's not around for long before we know he's bad news. When Frank arrives, Carla is feeling disorganised at work without her assistant Michelle who has gone on a cruise with Ciaran. Carla says that she needs someone with common sense to work for her, so why she offers the job to Maria, who can't walk and chew gum is anyone's guess. However, we soon find out that when it comes to dealing with fishy Frank Foster, what Carla was after by hiring Maria wasn't common sense after all, but a pretty face and a smile.

When the business deal with Frank is almost done, all that remains is for a sample of the product to be delivered to his flat. Carla hands this task to Maria and gives her the afternoon off work to tart herself up ready to conduct contract negotiations round at Frank's flat. However, when Maria gets to his place, Frank tries it on with her. He pushes too far, much too far and Maria flees, crying attempted rape.

The following day at the factory, Maria is quiet. Everyone else is over the moon that their jobs are safe after Frank rings Carla to accept the contract. When Frank eventually turns up at Underworld looking like butter wouldn't melt, he gets Maria alone. She accuses him of attempted rape and he apologises to her for 'misreading the signs'.

Maria comes clean to Carla about Frank. Although Carla is supportive and wants to bring in the police, they have no evidence of attempted rape. It would be Frank's word against Maria's and they decide not to call the cops. Instead, Carla confronts Frank herself. He says that he thought Maria had tarted herself up especially for him and he felt flattered. It's exactly what Carla had planned and she's left feeling guilty about the way she secured Frank's deal.

Frank then decides he wants to buy into Underworld. Maria is furious when she finds out. She walks out of Underworld in a huff and before she leaves, she slaps Carla across the face for going into business with the creep.

Carla's business problems with Frank and Maria are put to one side when she gets a call to say her mum Sharon has died. She handles the news the only way she knows how and orders a whole bottle of red in the Rovers. Frank takes her home after she's drunk too much and tucks her up in a blanket on the sofa.

Frank's caring side comes out again and impresses Carla no end. At the homeless shelter Roof & Refuge, Sophie and Sian plan an auction to raise charity funds. The event's held at Nick's Bistro and the movers and shakers of Weatherfield are there. They bid to win luxury items such as Deirdre's handmade pottery vase and a month of brunches at Roy's Rolls. Carla has her head turned by Frank when he bids £500 to win a handbag for her.

It's not long before the two of them become romantically entwined and Carla's doubts about Frank are pushed to the back of her mind. However, she still can't deny her feelings for Peter and the two of them meet in secret away from Frank and Leanne.

In the Rovers one night, Frank gets down on one knee and proposes to Carla with an enormous ring and a smirk on his face. Carla's less than impressed. 'This is a farce,' she snarls at him. 'Get up!'
And get up he does, determined to find out why Carla's turned him down. When he hears from Dev that Carla's been arguing with Peter in the shop, he figures things out. He guesses, correctly, that Carla's still got the hots for Peter and that's why she turned his proposal down. When he puts all this to Carla, she denies everything, even though it's all true. Still in denial over her true feelings for Peter, Carla finally agrees to marry Frank.

Frank's parents arrive for the party to celebrate their son's engagement. Carla takes an instant dislike to her prospective in-laws Anne and Sam. She gets drunk at the engagement party and tries to drive away from the Rovers in her car. However, she doesn't get very far before the car smashes into the bookies and mows down Stella Price. Both Stella and Carla are rushed to hospital but not until Frank moves Carla's body out of the driving seat. He's prepared to take the rap for Carla's car crash.

Carla recovers in hospital and the wheels are soon back in motion for her wedding to Frank. However, on the night before the wedding Carla's feelings for Peter overwhelm her and she confesses to Frank that she can't marry him. The two of them have a heated argument in her flat.

'But why?' Frank demands to know, even though he already knows the truth is that Carla's still in love with Peter.

' I just don't love you,' she says.

He demands to know if she's slept with Peter in their bed.

'In our bedroom? How many times?' he sneers.

'Stop it,' cries Carla.

'Every time you had a meeting with a so-called client, was he good, did he make you cry out?'

'Stop! It!' She screams. Carla walks to the door, unlocking it to get Frank to leave. He grabs her and locks the door, pushing her up against the door as Carla struggles to free herself. But she is no match for Frank who overpowers her and rapes her.

Afterwards, Carla is left helpless, lying on the floor, crying.

Frank stands over her. 'It's your fault,' he says. 'You made me do it, Carla…'

Then Frank walks towards the door and leaves. As soon as he's out of the flat, Carla locks the door behind him and slides down to the floor, crying. Distraught, she rings Maria who immediately calls the police.

The next morning, the residents of the street get dolled up in their best bib and tucker for Carla and Frank's wedding. The cake has arrived, the pink orchids are on the tables at the Bistro and Sally's got her fascinator on. But news soon spreads that the wedding is off. And it doesn't take long for the reason why to filter up the street, all the way to Peter. Peter spots Frank sneaking into the Bistro and thumps him so hard he falls into his own wedding cake. On what should have been his wedding day, Frank is arrested on suspicion of rape.

After the rape, Carla struggles. The ordeal causes her trouble sleeping and she goes to see her GP in the medical centre.
'I feel like a victim, and I don't do victim!' she tells Doctor Carter, who prescribes her sleeping pills.

Throughout all of this Peter supports Carla, his friend. At least he keeps telling himself, and anyone who'll listen, that Carla's his friend, just his friend. But there's more to it all and Leanne visits Frank in jail to find out what's really going on. She finds out more than she bargains for when Frank confesses it was Carla driving the car that crashed into her mum, Stella. Armed with this news, Leanne storms to Carla's flat where Peter is administering some TLC to the woman he still calls 'his friend'.

Still struggling to cope, Carla overdoses on her sleeping pills. She manages to ring Peter who saves her before she slips into a coma.

Later, in an effort to help her recover from the ordeal of the rape, Carla moves out of her flat and in with Maria and her son, little Liam. Finally Carla decides she's able to face going back to work. But when she walks into Underworld the first person she sees is Frank's mum, Anne. Anne tells Carla that she's got every right to be there, she's acting as proxy for her son.

Anne wastes no time at Underworld and strips out the fixtures and fittings, taking a share of everything she and her henchmen can lay their hands on. This leaves Carla with nothing to work with and she has no choice but to lay off her staff.

'But this job, it's the only thing that's, well, mine,' cries Sally with tears in her eyes when Carla sacks her. But Sally's tears soon dry when Frank's mum Anne poaches her and sets her to work for Frank in a rival firm to Carla's. It's another blow to Carla who's already been beaten down by the cops for harassing Frank when all she did was complain about his mum nicking her factory machines.

But after the trauma of the rape, losing her workforce, orders, machinists and money, Carla heads out to Los Angeles again. And while she's away the factory's saved by Michelle. Yes, Michelle! Michelle and Ciaran swan back to the street fresh from cruising around the world. By the time Carla returns from LA, Michelle has saved the factory, got Carla's machinists back to work and with Nick Tilsley's help has secured a new order too.

When Frank is released on bail he goes to see Carla, threatening her to drop the rape charges against him. 'I'm not some unreconstructed nut case,' he lies. 'It got out of hand between us, that's all.'

'You know what you are,' she hisses at him.

'Say the word,' he threatens her, up close to her face now.

Carla doesn't back down. 'Rapist,' she spits at him.

Frank picks up an empty bottle that Carla's recently polished off.

'Oh, look at that. You and Peter Barlow really do deserve each other, don't you? I can't believe that you fell for a lush. You're pathetic, Carla, you know that?'

He pretends to mimic Carla's voice: 'My name is Carla Connor and I'm an alcoholic. It's been twenty minutes since my last drink and I'm gasping for another.'

'I'd rather be an alcoholic than a rapist,' she snarls.

Meanwhile, Sally's full of herself at Frank's new factory where she gets all giddy in her power-dressing suit.

'I don't believe what Carla's saying about you,' she tells Frank, clearly overcome by the promise of a pay rise and a snog behind the sewing machine. In reward, Frank later sends Sally a text with a kiss at the end. It fair sends a blush right up Sally Webster's cheeks.

Since she returned from LA, Carla has been seeing Peter in secret, even though he's still with Leanne. They share a moment together and Peter gives Carla a necklace for her Christmas present. It's a necklace that Stella has already spied in Peter's shopping bag and assumed he'd bought for his wife.

Frank's mum Anne pays Carla another visit, this time at her flat. Anne says that if Carla drops the rape charges against Frank she can have Underworld back. It's blackmail of course. That's how desperate Anne is to save her son's reputation, but Carla isn't interested. When Carla finds out that Frank's hosting a drinks party at home for Underworld clients, she storms round intent on giving a speech and letting everyone know just how horrid Frank is. When the doorbell goes at the party, Sally rushes to answer. 'Sally,' Carla says, barging into the hallway. 'He's got you on the door, has he?'
She hands her jacket to Sally.
'Make yourself useful,' she says.
'She just barged in!' Sally moans as everyone turns to see the uninvited guest.
'Surprise!' Carla says before letting Frank's customers know just what a sleaze ball he is.

At the end of the night there's just Frank and Sally alone on the sofa with the red wine. He tells her the wine reminds him of her. 'It's strong yet delicate, with subtle undertones,' he coos as Sally leans in for a snog.

When Frank's rape trial begins, Carla, Maria and Peter are in court. Carla's in tears and Frank's got a sly grin on his face as he knows that his mum plans to stitch up Leanne. On the stand, the lawyer questions Peter and demands to know the answer to the question: 'Are you having a relationship with Carla Connor?'

Peter doesn't know want to say, not in front of his wife Leanne anyway. As Peter falters on the stand, Frank's mum Anne passes Leanne some photographs of Carla kissing Peter. They're photos that Frank's private detective has taken.
'Yes,' admits Peter, defeated. Leanne screams at him across the court room and then runs out in tears. Sadly for Carla, Frank is found not guilty of rape.

After the trial, back at Underworld, Frank makes Carla an offer she's very tempted to take. He wants the whole factory and plans to moves his workforce and his mum in. Carla thinks seriously about accepting Frank's offer, even if it is insultingly low. But when she goes to tell him she'll sell, Frank's nasty smirks and comments are too much to bear. She tells him to stick his offer for the knicker factory somewhere the gusset doesn't shine.

It's fair to say that Frank Foster has made few friends on Coronation Street. In fact, he's so despised that the vultures start circling around his head. Five suspects are lined up and given motives for bumping him off!

Will it be Sally when she finds out that Frank's having a fling with his business partner Jenny Sumner? Could it be Peter: 'I'll kill him stone cold dead. If ever a man deserved to die, it's him,' Barlow? Or maybe it's Kevin 'I'll kill him, I'll rip him apart with my bare hands,' Webster. Or maybe it's Carla herself or even Michelle who do Frank in for being a beast? Sally, Carla, Michelle, Peter and Kevin - these are the five suspects in the murder of evil Frank Foster when his body is found stone cold dead on the factory floor.

There are lights flashing, cops swarming and Norris gawping. Norris is even handing out bon-bons in exchange for gossip from anyone who knows anything. Carla's hauled to the cop shop as her fingerprints are found all over the whisky bottle that's been used to kill Frank. Unable to bear the possibility that Carla might have murdered Frank, Peter turns himself into the cops and tells them he did it.

After Frank's funeral takes place, Sally discovers that Anne is the one who killed Frank. Yes, Anne Foster killed her own son, that's how horrid the fella truly was. After Frank's death, Sally offers to buy Frank's share of the factory when it comes up for sale. While Carla doesn't need the aggravation of working alongside Sally in her power suit, she does need the money.
'In a lot of ways,' Sally muses, 'I'm the answer to Carla's prayers.'

As Sally fusses over the frillies, Michelle and Carla swap looks over the sewing machines, looks that suggest Sally's stash of cash will be more welcome in the factory office than Sally ever will. Sally goes all giddy kipper and gets ideas above her station when she gatecrashes a meeting that Carla's having with a customer in the Bistro.

'You need to open your mind!' Sally tells Carla.

'And you need to keep your gob shut!' Carla replies.

Not only is Sally's gob well and truly shut, she's gobsmacked when Frank's will is read. The will leaves Frank's Underworld shares to Carla. The factory is once again under her total control.

Rob Donovan

Carla's soon got more to worry about when her half-brother Rob turns up. He's just been freed from jail after serving eight years for armed robbery. Carla takes him on at the factory and under supervision of his big sister Rob takes on Eva Price as a new machinist. Eva's new to the sewing world and is all fingers and thumbs. Fortunately for Eva, they're not the body parts Rob's interested in.

Now that Carla and Peter's relationship has been exposed after the court case, they take a break to Los Angeles together. While they're away, Rob moves into Carla's flat. With Peter away, his sister Tracy takes control at the Bookies. Rob and Tracy are as devious as each other and make a perfect pair. When Peter and Carla return from the States, they learn that Leanne and Nick are about to be wed overseas. Relaxed after his holiday to California, Peter's very laid-back, giving a sly smirk where once he'd have let rip with his fists and a few choice words after a bottle or two.

Leanne decides she can't leave Simon with Peter while she jets away to get wed and so cancels the wedding. Nick rearranges it for Christmas day in Weatherfield instead. With all the talk of Leanne's wedding, Carla starts to realise that there's still a spark between Peter and Leanne. She handles things the only way she knows how.

She reaches for the bottle and drowns her sorrows, again, before heading back to LA. Nick also notices Leanne growing close again to Peter and he gets a face on him like a wet weekend in Wigan. Peter seems happy to play the long game in getting back with Leanne. He starts by getting close again to Simon, who's happy to have his dad back in his life.

On Leanne's hen night to her wedding to Nick, Eva tries to get Leanne so wrecked on booze that she won't be able to get up the next morning to face her wedding. Eva knows that it's Peter who Leanne loves, not Nick. But Leanne gets up just fine on the morning of the wedding. And then it all goes downhill. En route to the church in the back of a taxi, Leanne stops the cab to call at Peter's house. She offers him one last chance to be with her. If Peter says yes, Leanne's prepared to call off her wedding to Nick.

Peter was almost ready to take Leanne back. He had suggested as much to her the night before as he tried to snog her in the back room of the pub when Leanne came back from her hen do, all smudged mascara and tiara skew-whiff. And Peter was tempted, oh yes, he was tempted to say yes to Leanne. But in between Peter declaring undying love for Leanne in the back of the pub and Leanne offering herself to him in her wedding frock and bolero, something has changed. Something has happened. Someone has returned from Los Angeles.

Yup, Carla's back and Peter's head has been turned once again. Leanne lets rip at Carla, yelling at her that she'll only ever be Peter's second choice - but Carla already knows.

Over at Underworld, Rob decides to buy the factory when Carla tells him she wants to sell up. But he hasn't got the cash so he phones a few dodgy friends to see if they want to invest. Rob starts to cook the books to make Underworld appear less valuable than it is so that he can go in with a low offer to buy it from Carla. When Carla discovers what he's up to, she sacks Rob on the spot. Rob's shenanigans continue as he undercuts his sister and Carla ends up having to offload a knicker order that Rob has stolen from her. The only way Carla can get rid of the stock is to sell the pants cheap on the market to Nobby and Nolene. Now there's a couple we just have to meet.

Out for revenge on Peter after he snubbed her and went back to Carla, Leanne demands that Peter buy her out of Barlow's Bookies. Carla gives Peter the money to buy Leanne out of the business. She then installs Rob at the bookies to work with Peter, who doesn't want him there.

It's odds-on that Rob is going to rub Peter up the wrong way in the bookies. Peter lays a £20 bet with Steve that Rob won't last more than a week before he's running back to the knicker factory and swapping betting slips for under-slips.

Peter's right. Carla takes Rob back on at the factory after his stint at the bookies. She gives him a new role as Head of Distribution in the packing department with Kirk. He's not best pleased to be working there but when he finds out that fellow factory worker Tracy has to pick up an order of £20,000 pounds worth of silk, Rob hits on a devious plan.

Rob asks Tracy if she'll join him in his dodgy deal to steal the silk from his sister and Tracy agrees. She hands over the silk in a back alley to a dodgy geezer Rob knows and then gives herself a split lip and torn top to make it look like she's been robbed. Carla knows Tracy and Rob are lying when they spin her a yarn about the silk. At first, though, Carla isn't sure if Tracy really is daft enough to give herself a split lip. Peter soon puts her straight and lets Carla know that Tracy once ironed her own arm. She'd done it to make people think that Charlie Stubbs was abusing her.

Rob and Tracy continue to steal silk from Carla and they hide it in a lock-up. Carla does some ringing around and finds out from Sandra at Saunders of Sunderland that a woman has been on the phone offering silk for sale at a knock down price. Carla tells Sandra to arrange to meet this mystery woman, who turns out to be Tracy, of course. Later, Rob's expecting Sandra from Saunders of Sunderland to turn up for a business meeting. But tipped off by Sandra, it's Carla who turns up and finds her stolen silk. In exchange for not turning Rob into the cops, Carla tells her brother that she wants his shares of Underworld back.

'Sign up or go down,' she growls, proving she's got the size of balls that her brother can only dream of. So, not only does Rob fall out with his sister, he also loses his job and his factory shares.

Rob's paid off by Carla with a cheque to get him out of Underworld. Taking some of his pay-off cash to the bookies, he bets £500 on a four horse accumulator. Three horses win but the final one doesn't and the relief on Peter's face, well, it doesn't last long as there's a steward's enquiry and all four of Rob's horses win – to the tune of £35,190. It's not a tune that's sweet music to Peter's ears as it means Barlow's Bookies end up bankrupt.

However instead of seeing Peter lose the betting shop, Carla gives Rob some cash to keep him sweet, but it's nowhere near enough to cover the win. Peter ends up giving the bookies shop to Rob in exchange for paying his win on the horses.

When Deirdre finds out that Rob's bet on the horses was paid for with money Tracy stole from Amy's bank account, she's livid. Speaking of Deirdre, she consoles Carla after she has a fall out with Peter. Deirdre tells her she can offer neutral opinion. 'Just think of me as Switzerland in glasses.'

Peter Barlow

Carla decides to ask Peter to become her partner – in life and in business.

'Make an honest woman of me,' she tells him. 'You know how Deirdre likes a good wedding.' The two of them announce their engagement and go shopping for a sparkler.

As their wedding plans begin, Carla decides to employ Peter at the factory. The problem is, he knows nothing about knickers or office politics. He upsets Michelle so wonderfully at work one day that she walks out and takes a job at the Rovers instead. When Carla returns from a business trip to Antwerp she tries, but fails, to get Michelle back.

Managing Peter at work is one thing, but if Carla thinks she can control Peter outside of the office, she's got another thing coming. Their problems begin when he employs Tina McIntyre as Simon's baby-sitter. The little lad is still trying to cope with being passed from Nick and Leanne to Peter and Carla. It doesn't take long before Peter decides he'd like a bit of sitting on the naughty step with his son's babysitter, too.

Meanwhile, Hayley cracks on with designing Carla's wedding dress. It's got puffed sleeves and frills and Carla's not best pleased. She is not, after all, a puffed sleeves and frills girl. Moaning to Peter in the factory, Carla wonders if asking Hayley to design her wedding dress was a good idea.

So it's back to the drawing board as Carla rips up Hayley's design. She makes her own design, sticking bits of paper together, matching bits from one frock design with another.

'Can you make it?' Carla asks Hayley.

'Yes I can!' Hayley replies.

Hayley puts the finishing touches to Carla's wedding dress and takes it into the factory for Carla to see.

'Do you like it?' asks Hayley.

'No, I don't like it,' Carla replies. 'I don't like it one bit. I love it!'

On the night before the wedding Peter's almost driven to drink but is saved by the doorbell when Tina turns up. The two of them have a heart to heart before Carla returns and stops them from getting to know each other a little bit more.

On her wedding day, Carla looks lovely in her frock made by Hayley and is walked down the aisle by her brother, Rob.

She turns to Peter to say her vows.

'I promise to be there when you need me. I promise to help you be the best you can be. I promise to accept you for who you are and to love you always in good times and in bad.'

Peter admits that he's no good at public speaking and reveals he found his speech on the internet.

'Now you will feel no rain,' he tells Carla. 'Because I will be your shelter. Now you will feel no cold for I will keep you warm. And I thought 'yes, that's it', because that's how I feel. I want to look after you because you make me a better man and I promise to love you above all other people.'

There's not a dry eye in the house after that speech, but Tina looks very uncomfortable indeed. The registrar ends the ceremony with: 'I now pronounce you husband and wife. You may kiss if you like.' Oh, and they do like! Peter grabs Carla and dips her to kiss her as their guests give a round of applause. But when the partying starts at the reception, Carla ends up having way too much to drink. Peter takes her up to the bridal suite where she falls fast asleep on their wedding bed. As Carla snores away upstairs, Peter and Tina end up snogging downstairs after the wedding guests have gone home.

When Peter and Carla return from honeymoon in Bali, Peter carries Carla over the threshold - at Underworld. Tina wants to take up where she left off with Peter before he married Carla. But Peter tells Tina to cool it.

The newly-married Carla Barlow has much on her mind after she returns from honeymoon. Hayley is taken ill and Carla insists on accompanying her to the hospital for her scan. She supports her friend as much as she can. In the hospital waiting room, Carla asks Hayley:
'What's yours and Roy's secret, Hayley?'
'I don't know,' Hayley replies. 'We don't really have any common interests.'
'No, me and Peter don't on the surface. It's not about the surface though, is it?'

When the nurse comes to call Hayley in to see the consultant, Hayley tells Carla to head back to work. 'You get back now Mrs Connor, I'll be fine.'
'No, I'm staying,' Carla says.
'No, really. You've done enough, I'll see you later. '
'Oh, OK, well, good luck, call me if you need me, won't you?'
'I'll be fine,' says Hayley.

Sadly, Hayley's not fine. She's not fine at all. She's given the devastating news that she has pancreatic cancer, and breaks down at work in the factory one day. With the news of her diagnosis playing heavy on her mind, she keeps the news to herself. The factory girls have no idea what's going on, and Beth's loud mouth becomes too much for Hayley, who breaks down in tears. Carla sees what's going on through her office window and rescues Hayley. She calls out to the factory floor.
'Hayley! I need you to check something in here! NOW!'
Hayley runs into the office and as soon as she's in and sitting down, Carla closes the blinds and locks the door. Hayley breaks down and cries: 'They've found a tumour…'

Hayley's then given the heartbreaking news that she's only got weeks left to live. The news filters around the street after she and Roy agree that friends should be told. Roy takes his shopping bag and goes to break the news to Carla in the flat. Carla demands to see Hayley, barges across the street and into Roy's flat. She heads straight to Hayley's bedroom and gets into bed with her for a cosy little chat.

While Carla's out visiting Hayley, Tina turns up at Carla's flat, barges into the bedroom and gets into bed with Peter for a cosy little chat … and more. But Roy then realises he's left his bag at Carla's flat! He heads back and gives Peter palpitations when Peter hears someone at the front door and thinks Carla's returned.

So it's a close shave for Peter and Tina. At the Rovers, Tina confides in Liz she's having a fling with a married man. Liz isn't daft, she knows what's going on and threatens Peter in the men's loo at the Rovers to stay away from Tina. Tina's all over the place, not knowing where she is with Peter who is still declaring his undying love for Carla. Tina decides to leave Weatherfield and trundles off to that London with a pink suitcase and a scowl in the back of a cab. Carla's none the wiser about what Peter's been up to.

Carla's heart breaks when news reaches her that Hayley has died. At Hayley's funeral the mourners all wear a splash of colour, as Hayley had requested and Carla turns up in a bright red suit. Roy doesn't think he can go through with the service, and it's left to Carla and Fiz who gently persuade him to leave the flat.

Carla heads off to Paris on a business trip leaving Peter home alone in the flat just long enough for him to get Tina in again for sub-duvet shenanigans. He then hops on a plane to Paris to be with his wife, telling Tina they'll get together on his return and see how things go. Tina begs Peter to leave Carla but Peter just wants Tina as his 'bit on the side'.

When Peter returns early from Paris he and Tina snuggle up again in bed celebrating Tina's birthday. But Steve and Lloyd spot a light on up in the flat. They reckon it's burglars as they believe Peter's still in Paris and so they get the spare keys from Michelle and enter the flat to find out what's going on. What they find is more than they expect – it's Tina in her birthday suit! She grabs her clothes, covers up and lies through her teeth about using Carla's shower as her boiler's gone off.

On her return from Paris, Carla takes a pregnancy test and is shocked to discover that she's pregnant. Peter gets very, very drunk after Carla tells him the news. What Carla doesn't know is that Tina has told Peter she thinks that she's pregnant too. This double pregnancy news would be enough to drive anyone to drink and it knocks Peter over the edge and into the nearest pub. Steve goes to collect him to bring him home but realises he can't take Peter home in such a drunken state. And so, Steve and Peter stay overnight in a bed and breakfast. The morning after the night before, the two lads wake up in bed together. Peter realises that he's got a hangover the size of Weatherfield itself, and worse still, that he's confessed to Steve about both his wife Carla and his fancy-piece Tina being pregnant by him.

The two fellas go home with a story they've concocted about Steve being the one who was the worse for wear with drink.

Steve has to pretend he's hungover all day, while Peter gets the shakes from his very real hangover. He pledges, again, never to succumb to drinking, again, but they are empty words. Tina pops round with a pregnancy test and to Peter's relief he finds out she's not pregnant. But Tina's distraught.

'I wanted our baby,' she cries.

Peter dumps her… slowly and carefully, but definitely, and she leaves the flat, telling her flatmate Steph later at home:

'If he thinks he can live happily ever after… he's got another thing coming!'

While Peter nurses another hangover up in the flat, Carla doesn't want him left alone in case he starts drinking again. She brings in Steve to babysit Peter and this is news that makes Rob laugh.

'It's like leaving a monkey in charge of the bananas!' Indeed, the only thing worse than leaving Peter with Steve is leaving Peter with Tina. But that's exactly what Carla goes and does when she changes babysitting shifts and brings in Tina to look after Peter. Deirdre wonders what's going on with Peter that he would start again on the booze. She is curious to know whether Carla's got money trouble, to which Tracy replies: 'Carla's got handbags worth more than your house!'

In an effort to help Peter off the booze, his family send him into rehab, again. When he's back home, Peter meets Tina in a hotel bar while Carla's waiting for him at hospital to have her baby scan. When Tina nips to the ladies on the way out of their clandestine meeting at the hotel, Rob walks in.

He spots Peter looking furtive in the hotel foyer. Rob knows Peter's up to no good and Peter's sweating in case Tina comes out of the ladies while Rob's there. But Tina comes out after Rob has moved on, and Peter breathes a sigh of relief. He drops Tina off in a taxi and then gets absolutely bladdered, again. He forgets all about Carla who has her baby scan done at the hospital, alone.

When Carla gets back to the flat she's upset and angry. She waits for Peter to return home and when he finally does come in, he's drunk, very drunk.
'I thought you'd be in bed,' Peter slurs when he comes in through the door.
'Really?' Carla asks him. 'You think I could get my head down with you out god knows where? Where have you been Peter? And don't even think about lying!'
'Can't you guess?' he says. 'Can't you see? Do you really need me to spell it out?'
'Yes I do. Because unless you spell it out for me I don't think I can believe it. When I was looking at our baby for the first time, for the very first time Peter, you were… come on, that's your cue!'
'Drinking, I was out drinking.'
'So come on then, did you even intend on coming to the scan?'
'No it wasn't like that. It's complicated,' he lies.
'It's not complicated, not really,' Carla says.
'I'm so…' he starts to say, but Carla cuts him short.
'Don't you dare say you're sorry!'
Carla's rage and frustration comes walloping out of her, she hits Peter, she thumps him and he's on his knees in front of her, crying his drunken eyes out.

'There's no hope for us is there?' she yells at him. 'What hope is there... if today of all days you couldn't stop yourself from having a drink? If me and this baby inside me aren't enough for you we have no chance, we have not one chance.'
Carla flings the scan of their unborn baby at him. 'Our beautiful baby - in case you're interested.'
Peter falls to the floor, sobbing, unable to control himself.

Rob's suspicions about Peter deepen when he spies Peter chatting to Tina in the Rovers, He then sees Tina using a pen emblazoned with the name of the hotel he found Peter in. Rob soon figures out what's going on between Peter and Tina.

Aware that Rob's on his case, Peter confesses to Carla about his fling with Tina. Later, Carla confronts Tina in the street.
'Carla...!' Tina cries, shocked to see her.
'Carla?' she mimics back and laughs in Tina's face.
'What? You're sorry? You're sorry it ever happened? You're sorry you kissed my husband on my wedding night?'
'If you didn't get drunk and passed out, none of this would have happened,' says Tina.
'Oh, I'm sorry. It's the butterfly effect,' replies Carla. 'So... what? I pass out. You copped off with Peter. Peter dumped you and I found out, eh? Eh, Tina? The question is, you backstabbing little tramp - what next?'

While Carla and Peter drift apart after his affair is exposed, Rob and Tracy grow close. They decide to get wed and throw an engagement party in the Rovers. But while the party is in full swing, Rob and Tracy both sneak out, separately, unnoticed. Tracy has promised to drive a van full of knock-off goods for Tony Stewart. And Rob goes to see Tina. He tells her he knows about her affair with his brother-in-law and demands that she leaves Peter alone. And while Rob is there with Tina in her flat, she falls from the balcony to the cobbles below. When Rob leaves the flat to check on Tina's body down on the cobbles, she's still alive, just. Tina rises to her feet and gives Rob a verbal lashing that only Tina could give.
'You're gobby,' Rob says.
'I was born gobby!' she yells.
Rob spies a piece of lead piping in the builders' yard and takes it, whacks Tina with it and this time, leaves her for dead. Tina is rushed to hospital and fights for her pretty life in intensive care with tubes up her nose and Rita by her side. It's not looking good and Tina loses her fight for life.

News of Tina's murder spreads and gossip is rife. Peter's suspect number one and is determined to prove his innocence, but being permanently drunk is getting in his way. Rob does his best to cover his guilty tracks and fights as much as he can with Peter, winding him up and pointing the finger of blame his way. It's too much for Carla, the stress gets to her and she collapses in pain before being rushed to hospital where she miscarries her baby.

Roy is one of Carla's first visitors and is apprehensive as he enters her hospital room. Carla's sitting up in her bed wearing blue striped pajamas.

'I can easy come back,' he says.

'No, come in.'

Roy sits by the side of her bad.

'I'm having a bad hair day,' she jokes.

'I'm sorry you lost the baby,' says Roy, coming straight out with it. He passes her a white cotton handkerchief.

'Here, one of Hayley's. I thought it might bring you some comfort.'

Carla accepts the handkerchief, dissolving into tears.

'I'm glad you came,' she says, finally.

'Life can be cruel and arbitrary, but you already know that.'

'Yeah, so do you.'

'There's no point in trying to summon a fresh thought, something profound, cast the tragedy in a new light. I think you would have made an excellent mother.'

'I think you're in a minority of one there. It was a girl,' Carla tells him, dissolving into tears again. 'She was a little girl.'

Roy holds Carla's hand. 'I'm so sorry.'

'She chose to opt out, just pressed the eject button, you know. I don't blame her. I really loved her, you know once I got my head around the idea, I really loved her. Every night, every morning, come on you're doing great, a little bit bigger, getting stronger. She's gone. Everything's gone.'

Rob and Michelle determine to keep things ticking over at the factory for Carla. But when they're in there sorting papers, in walks Peter, determined to get his share of the factory and to win Carla back. Peter's still suspect number one in the hunt for Tina's murderer and the police have Carla under suspicion too. Rob does his utmost to stop Peter seeing Carla but Peter takes his chance when he spies Carla on the cobbles, drunk. The two of them go up to the flat and get stuck into a bottle of red wine that Carla's been keeping at the back of the wardrobe. Drunk, the two of them start arguing about Tina.

'Why did you do it?' Carla demands to know.
'What?' Peter asks.
'What? You're always hedging your bets with me. What's Carla going to ask me next? "Did I kill her"?'
'I didn't kill her, She…'
'Don't!' Carla yells at him. 'Don't you dare blame her…'
'I'm not, I'm not!'
'Don't blame anybody else but yourself.'
'I should be dead.' Peter slurs. 'It should be me that's dead.'
'Hell yeah. I'll do a soft shoe shuffle on your grave, an' all. I'm going to prison. You know what? I can feel it. Prison. And what for? Being cheated on, humiliated, losing my baby.'
Peter stands and tries to comfort Carla but she bats him away.
'Don't you touch me! Don't you dare touch me! I never wanted a baby. You made me want it, you made me care. She's better off dead where she is.'
'No,' cries Peter.

'Half you, half me.'

'No!'

'A monster.'

'No, Carla! No!'

'A freak. How could I have ever loved her … half of you? I hate you,' she cries.

'I'm sorry,' Peter slurs. 'Just let me help you...' and he reaches over to Carla but again she pushes him away. The two of them start fighting.

'I hate you… I hate you,' she yells, hitting Peter over and over.

'I love you,' he cries.

The two of them fall into each other's arms and kiss. Carla pulls away from the kiss immediately.

'You should be dead,' she tells Peter. 'Not Tina. Not my baby. Not my baby!'

Peter tries to comfort her again, but Carla pushes him away and he falls back onto the sofa. Just at the moment, Rob comes into the flat, shocked to see Peter there.

'What the hell is he doing here?' Rob shouts.

Peter whispers to Carla: 'I love you,' just as Rob grabs hold of him and chucks him towards the door.

'I didn't kill Tina and I don't believe you did, either,' Peter says before he leaves. 'You've still got feelings for me - or why kiss me?'

'So you can see what you chucked away!' Carla shouts at him. 'Summat you'll never, ever have again.'

Rob's heard enough and pushes Peter through the door. 'I said GET OUT!' then slams the door behind him.

Incredulous, Rob turns to his sister. 'You kissed him?'

The next morning, Peter returns to see Carla to apologise for his behaviour the night before.

'Get out,' she tells Peter

'I need to talk to you.'

'That's not the impression you gave last night. What do you want?'

'You,' he says. 'I didn't kill Tina and deep down I think you know that.'

'Oh you think that's all right do you? Cheating on me from day one? Giving you a job, picking you up while you were in the gutter? While I was pregnant! You think we can just wipe the slate clean and start again?'

Peter sighs. 'I've learned my lesson.'

'I gave you everything, Peter. Every last bit of me. Bits that I didn't even know were there.'

'I've never stopped loving you, Carla, it's true, despite everything that's happened. And I know that you don't deserve it but that's how I feel.'

She walks to the door to get him to leave.

'Just. Get. Out.'

'Last night…,' he starts to say but Carla cuts him short.

'Last night I was drunk. I wanted you to want me. I wanted you to feel weak, that's all that was.'

'Look me in the eyes and tell me you don't love me,' Peter pleads.

'I wish it was you that was dead.'

Peter turns and leaves the flat and Carla slams the door shut behind him.

Rob's so far managed to keep himself distanced from the murder of Tina. He does his best to pin her death on Peter every chance he can. Then Rob spots Tracy wearing a bracelet that Eccles sniffed out in the backyard at the Barlows. It's a bracelet that he took from Tina's flat on the night she died, in an attempt to make her death look like it was part of a bungled break-in. Rob comes out in a cold sweat, more so when Steph in the Bistro challenges Tracy as to why she's wearing her bracelet. The next thing you know, the cops are crawling all over the cobbles. They deduce that whoever stole the bracelet must be the same person who killed Tina. Fortunately for Rob, Deirdre cleaned the bracelet when Eccles found it and his fingerprints aren't on it. Unfortunately for Peter, who has touched the bracelet more recently, his are. He's arrested and jailed for the murder of Tina. When Ken returns from an extended break to Canada, he's furious to find out that Peter's in prison and Deirdre hasn't told him. Ken finds out from Carla who takes him for a drink and fills him in on all the bad news.

Carla packs up and leaves Peter's flat and moves up in the world, to her own flat in Victoria Court. Her wine glasses are the last things to be packed and the first to be unwrapped in her new home.

When Tracy and Rob's wedding day dawns, Rob asks Carla to be his best man. Tracy turns up for her wedding in a horse-drawn carriage – and she arrives just in time to see Rob do a runner.

He's running because Carla tells him she's had no choice but to call the police. She knows her brother killed Tina. Rob begs her not to turn him into the cops but she isn't prepared to let him get away with the crime.

With Peter in the clear when Rob gets arrested, he decides to leave Weatherfield. Sitting on Maxine's bench with Simon, Peter tells his son he's leaving for Portsmouth. Just then, Carla walks by and sits on the bench with them both. She puts her arm around Simon, knowing how upset he'll be to hear the news that his dad's leaving, again.

'You think I'm a right cow don't you?' she asks Simon
'Yeah,' says Simon.
'Hey, hey, don't….' says Peter, but Carla interrupts him.
'No it's all right, he's just being honest, it's good to be honest. Can I be honest with you, Si? I didn't like you much when I first met you.'
'Why?' he asks.
'Why? Because you were a right little know-it-all with this angelic little face that knew how to get my goat and wind me round your little finger.'
Carla pulls Simon closer to her.
'Now I have got to know you, I've grown dead fond of you and although things have worked out a bit, well, rubbish really between me and your dad, I'd cut my own arm off to save you from misery, you know that.'

'Then why are you making him go?' Simon cries.

'She's not, Si,' says Peter. 'I have to go mate, because I'm a mess. I've got to sort my head out, you know the drinking and what happened with me and Tina and all the pain that I've caused people, you included. That's not right, is it? I have to go because I have to know why I'm like that. Away from the people that I've caused pain to.'

'You see me?' says Carla. 'I get on a plane to America and go thousands of miles away. Your dad's only going down south. And I always come back. Your dad will too.'

'Will you?' asks Simon.

'Of course,' Peter replies.

'And I'm going to make you a promise right now,' Carla says. 'In them summer holidays if you're missing him so much I'm going to put you on a train, or better still in a cab with Steve or Lloyd and you'll be with him before you know it.'

'Will you come too?' Simon asks.

'No, but I'll pay your fare. Portsmouth. Please... can you really see me in Portsmouth?'

'Do you promise?' he asks again.

'I've said, haven't I?'

Carla kisses Simon on the head, stands and walks away from the bench.

'Hey!' Peter says. She stops and turns towards her ex.

'See you then,' he smiles.

'Not if I see you first,' she smiles back.

All change at Underworld

Over at Underworld, Alya Nazir is interviewed for
the role of office manager under Carla's supervision.
Alya waffles on about designer lingerie, finest
Austrian lace and sumptuous silk. When Carla asks
her what she thinks about cheap polyester pants,
Alya bristles until Carla points out that they're what
keeps Underworld going. Alya's on a steep learning
curve, but Carla takes her on.

Carla and Michelle head off for a girly day at a spa.
The ladies warm to hunky spa receptionist Claudio
who tells them he'll be their masseur for the day
along with his colleague Phil. Carla can barely hide
her delight then isn't best pleased when she finds out
that Phil is Philomena. Still, Carla and Michelle
soldier on at the spa, enjoying massage and face-
masks. Carla's chilled out back on the cobbles but it
doesn't last long when she finds out someone's
broken into the factory and smashed the place up.
She's even more furious when she finds out who it is.
Distraught over Rob being arrested for Tina's
murder, Tracy has been into the factory and caused
as much damage as she possibly can.

Carla walks into the factory to face Tracy. The two of
them argue and fight on the factory floor. Finally,
they calm down and have a heart-to-heart.
'You've got money,' Tracy tells Carla. 'The factory,
your own flat.'
Carla pauses.
'You've got Amy,' she replies wistfully.

Carla's keen to put things behind her and she offers to pay Tracy's wedding debts to Michelle. Carla hopes they can move on now with their lives, but Tracy gets a smirk on her face, planning her next move.

In the office at Underworld, Alya answers the phone to be told that Carla's been nominated in the North West Fashion Trade Awards. There's a free bar at the do, a free meal and a disco. And there's a mini-bus load of Underworld employees excited to be attending to see Carla win her prize. Alya sets about with a clipboard collecting names for the mini-bus and Sally's not best pleased she wasn't given this task.

The Underworld girls and Sean all gather on the bus in their best bib and tucker for the outing to the do. Steve's driving the bus and gets into a spot of road rage with boy racers on a quiet country lane, close to a cliff edge. The bus is run off the road, crashes, rolls upside down on its roof and ends up hanging over a cliff edge with the Underworld staff stuck inside. Steve's first out of the bus, he can't handle what's happened and takes himself away, in shock. Michelle's next out and comforts him, only too aware that Steve's blaming himself. Slowly but surely everyone else clambers, or crawls, out of the wreckage in various states of shock and distress with cuts and bruises all over. All the while, the bus creaks and moans with the shifting weight inside it, barely hanging on to the cliff edge as everyone gets out alive, Sinead only just.

But there's no sign of Carla, she's still inside, stuck at the front of the bus. The bus is now dangling over the cliff edge, threatening to break free and tumble to destruction at any second. It's Tracy who goes back to free Carla and becomes the heroine of the hour, much to Carla's relief - and disdain.

'I had my life saved by Tracy-flaming-Barlow!' Carla cries

Nick Tilsley

Carla changes her name from Barlow, legally and officially, to her first married surname of Connor. And when she returns from another break in Los Angeles she soon becomes cosy with Nick in her flat. When he pops round to fix her laptop the two of them bond over business and cake. Nick has much on his mind when he starts falling for Carla and she starts falling back. They fall together so much they even meet in the middle and kiss, that is, until Erica Holroyd gives Nick a baby bombshell and tells him she's pregnant with his child.

Nick cools things with Carla and tells Erica he wants her and the baby to move into his flat. But then Nick's got more thinking to do as he falls deeper for Carla and the two of them share a snog on the street. Sadly, Erica suffers a miscarriage and loses the baby. After Erica's miscarriage, Nick tells Carla it's her he wants to be with. He calls at her flat and lays his heart on the line.

'There's only one thing wrong with Erica,' he whispers.

'One thing? Only one thing? Well, I think I'll settle for one thing, Nicholas,' she replies. 'So what is it? This one thing?'

Nick leans in for a kiss and tells Carla: 'She's not you.'

As a favour to Liz one night, Carla takes Amy up to her flat to look after her overnight. She gives Amy her bed and Carla takes the sofa. In the middle of the night, Tracy breaks into Carla's flat with Michelle's keys that she's nicked from her handbag. Tracy seems intent on killing Carla. She lifts a heavy ornament over her head as Carla snores on the sofa … but decides not to kill her that way. Has she had a change of heart? She then lights a candle and finds a picture of Rob. Unaware that Amy is also in the flat, Tracy's startled when she hears the toilet flush, and she runs out, leaving the candle burning and burning … and Victoria Court goes up in flames.

As the fire rages in Carla's flat, Leanne notices the flames from outside and tries to break into the flat using a fire extinguisher to bash open the door. Carla is freed but she's overcome by smoke and unable to speak. She isn't able to let anyone know that Amy's inside. Roy uses his first aid skills to help Carla until the ambulance arrives, but … Oh! No! … the ambulance is stuck on the ring road. Finally, Carla can breathe, just enough to whisper one word – Amy! Kal and Leanne rush back into the flat to save Amy's life. But by now the whole of Victoria Court is up in flames, with a gas canister on a balcony threatening to blow. Leanne manages to free herself but it's too late for Kal. He's caught in the blast and dies. Down at the builders' yard the fire rages there too and Maddie Heath dies, trapped in the flames.

Everyone blames Carla for the fire and the deaths and she does her best to keep a low profile, along with Roy's help. One evening Roy is locking up the café while looking after Carla, telling her over and over that the fire wasn't her fault.

'It was an accident,' says Roy.

'It was a mistake, Roy,' Carla cries, burying her head in her hands. 'It was my mistake.'

At that moment, Tracy Barlow swans in through the café door.

'We're closed,' Roy says, but Tracy ignores him.

'What for? Day of mourning?'

'What do you want?' asks Roy.

Tracy looks at Carla. 'I want to know how it feels to be responsible for so much suffering…'

'I'd like you to leave, please,' says Roy but Tracy's not finished with Carla just yet. She needs to pin as much blame on Carla as she can so that no blame for the fire can be pointed at her.

'Father, son, lover. So many people have got a whacking great hole in their life because of you! So many people despise you Carla and the air you breath. Yeah, well, welcome to my world. Let's see how you like it.'

Carla starts to spiral out of control with the guilt of Kal and Maddie's deaths on her mind. Roy's not happy when he walks into the café to find her gambling and drinking inside. She's set up a poker game with Erica, Nick and Lloyd.

Roy warns Carla she could have cost him his license. She continues to gamble and drink, staying out all night at a casino in town. Roy admonishes her the next day for coming home in the early hours. He knows what time it was, he tells her, because the shipping forecast was on the radio. She replies with: 'Shipping forecast … Shiraz … whatever gets you through the night, Roy.'

Carla struggles to cope and her retreat into gambling gets worse when she starts gambling online at work. Then she starts visiting the casino in town, spending her own cash and that from Underworld too. Unable to cope, Carla goes away on an overseas trip. She tells everyone that she's been to Madrid but she's been gambling in Las Vegas instead.

Not only has she been gambling all her own money but Underworld's accounts are over thirty thousand down too. Michelle, Nick and Roy stage an intervention in her flat. Carla knows she has to do something, but what? She tells the factory girls she's moving away and putting the factory up for sale. Sally gets her hopes up about buying the place. She opens the company accounts to see what state the books are in before she makes an offer. When Carla finds Sally at the computer looking at the accounts she sacks her on the spot.

'Drop dead!' Sally yells before walking out in a huff.

The horror of the guilt, thinking she caused two people to die in the fire, is proving too much to bear. Carla even steals Nick's credit card and starts gambling his money too. Michelle's exasperated and tells Carla to call a counsellor for help. But desperate Carla doesn't see a counsellor. She drives off to a quarry, determined to end her own life. Following her is Tracy Barlow. When she finds Carla standing on a cliff-edge with a bottle of booze in her hand, she edges behind Carla to hear what she's saying. She sees Carla throws a coin up into the air.

'Heads I stand. Tails I fall.'

'Carla! Wait!' Tracy yells. 'It wasn't you! You didn't leave the candle burning. Amy didn't get up in the night and light it. It was ME! I did it!'

'What are you saying? You weren't even there!'

'I was, I don't know what I was thinking, I just wanted to ...'

'You wanted to burn your own daughter to death?'

'No, no, she was supposed to be staying with Liz.'

'So me, then? Me? You wanted to burn me?'

'No. The fire was an accident. You Carla, you know you're like a magnet. You walk in a room and heads turn, money sticks to you and people, decent people, you know, not just family but people who should know better. Roy. Hayley. Even Maddie.'

'Tracy, what are you saying? What are you even saying? This is crazy. You don't try and kill someone because they're popular.'

'You had everything. Everything. And all I wanted was that pub.'

'The Rovers?'

'Yes the Rovers. Yes, me and Tony were made for it.'

'You lied and you ended up killing two people because you wanted a share in a backstreet pub?'
'You know it wasn't enough that you took Rob…'
'Rob took himself after he took Tina.'
'Well I'd had enough. I wanted to make you pay.'

The argument with Tracy, and hearing her confess to the fire, is enough to pull Carla back from the brink. She later repeats Tracy's confession in the pub. Tracy is there with Robert and also at the bar are Kal's children Zeedan and Alya. Carla glances at Tracy and says: 'I, er, I didn't start that fire, did I, Tracy?
'Oh… how much have you had to drink?' Tracy spits back, worried about where the conversation will go.
'You started the fire when you stole Michelle's keys and you broke into my flat and you lit that candle.'
Robert turns to Tracy. 'Is this true?,' he demands.
'No of course it's not true. She's off her head, everybody knows that.'
'Oh, it's true all right,' Carla says. 'She told me all about it, she confessed it to me yesterday. The guilt must be eating away at you.'
Alya rounds on Tracy, demanding to know what happened.
'Is it true? Our dad's dead because of you?'
Tracy starts to look worried. 'She's making it up and I don't need to listen to this.'
She picks up her bag and heads for the door. 'Come on Robert!'
Just at that moment, two policemen enter the Rovers.
'Tracy Barlow?' one of the cops ask. 'I'm arresting you on suspicion of murder.'

The Connors

As Carla's meltdown continues, Nick calls Aidan Connor, a distant cousin of Michelle's. He asks Aidan to come to Weatherfield to help out at Underworld. Aidan agrees in a heartbeat, he's only too happy to help.

Over at Underworld, having pulled herself together a little, Carla secures a new contract for comfortable bras. These are tested out by the client power-walking up and down the cobbles, checking for bounce. As Carla's securing the deal, Aidan's dad Johnny and his sister Kate walk into Underworld and into Carla's life. Johnny's not best pleased with his son for investing in Underworld with what, Carla discovers, are Johnny's life savings. Carla now has to negotiate which one of the Connor men she's running a business with. Is it the young and fashionable Aidan, the older and wiser Johnny - or both?

Johnny Connor quickly gets his feet under the table at Underworld. At first, he undermines Carla's authority by buying in cheap material from the back of a truck. But with Aidan's strategic help Johnny brings in an order, a big order that puts the girls and Sean on overtime and requires an additional pair of hands on the machines. The hands that are hired are perfectly manicured and belong to Eva, who's back working in the factory when Carla takes her back. Aidan isn't happy that Carla's hired someone without asking him first but when he sees Eva he fair falls in love.

However, the new Connor men aren't as keen on all their machinists and Johnny takes an instant dislike to Sally.

'It's her voice, it grates!' he tells Carla before suggesting they demote her from supervisor in the office to working back on the machines. Carla agrees to Johnny's demand.

While the Connors are running Underworld, Carla and Nick get engaged after Carla asks Nick to marry her. He then pops the same question back to her in front of their families in the Bistro.

'I've survived the Barlows, I'm sure I can survive the Platts,' Carla muses while being given the evil-eye by Gail.

However, being engaged to Nick doesn't run as smoothly as Carla would like. The disruption begins when Tracy receives a prison visiting order from Rob. Tracy dolls herself up for the prison visit where Rob sweet talks his ex. What he really wants to know is what's going on at Underworld. He's spotted a picture in the Weatherfield Gazette and read about Johnny Connor joining the knicker-stitching gang.

Another visiting order wings its way to Johnny who dons his dapper waistcoat to visit Rob in jail. Rob tells Johnny he knows he got their mam pregnant about nine months before Carla was born. Rob reckons that Johnny might be Carla's real dad.

Johnny agrees that he had a one-night fling with Carla's mam in the backseat of a Vauxhall Cavalier. But he defies Rob to show him proof that he's really Carla's dad. The fact that Johnny goes all shifty and sweaty provides Rob with all the proof that he needs. Rob plans to blackmail Johnny to keep the truth from Carla about who her real dad is. Johnny heads back to Coronation Street with much on his mind. He needs proof to show whether Carla's his daughter or not. He buys a DNA kit and sends it off in the post with an envelope that Carla's licked at work. When the results come back, he has all the proof that he needs.

Johnny needs to speak to Carla but finds it hard to pick the right moment. Finally, he gets her on her own and asks her to come back to the flat with him. Carla wonders what on earth's going on, but follows Johnny to the flat. He tells her he's got some news and she might want to sit down when she hears it. 'If you'd have known me back in the day,' Johnny begins, hesitantly. 'I mean…. as I said to Liz, if I could've got hold of the kid that I was, that idiot.' 'So whatever this is, Liz knows?' asks Carla, surprised that he's already told Liz.
'I'd handle it all differently. I was younger than our Aidan is now,' says Johnny sadly.
Carla starts to look uncomfortable.
'OK Johnny. Look, you're officially freaking me out OK. So either come out and say it, whatever it is or I'll save you the stress. I'll go and ask Liz. Come on, it's your call.'

'I don't want it to change everything, that's all. It doesn't have to, OK? Look at me,' he begs Carla. 'It doesn't have to.'
Carla stands, ready to walk out. 'Ok, I'll see Liz then.'
'No!' says Johnny, afraid he's going to lose her again. 'Ok. I'm your dad. Carla, I'm your dad.'

Carla doesn't take the news well. She starts drinking to excess, again, and goes to the casino for the afternoon. Joining her at the casino table is Robert Preston, who's there because he's had an argument with Tracy. Carla and Robert are a match made in hell, both fiery and alpha. Robert wins at the table and they celebrate with a bottle of bubbly which they take upstairs for a spot of how's-your-father. After she sleeps with Robert in the casino hotel room, Carla tells him it was a mistake, she was drunk, and she doesn't want it mentioning ever again.

In the back room of the Rovers, Connor clan secrets explode when Carla breaks Johnny's news to the rest of his family. Kate and Aidan are summoned there by Carla. Johnny, Liz and Nick are there too, all crowded around the dining table in the back room of the pub.
'Honestly, I didn't want to do this…' Carla says to Kate and Aidan. 'But you've got a right to know the truth.'
'Let me tell them myself, in private,' begs Johnny, but Carla's not moving on this.
'Johnny, it needs to be now.'
'No, it doesn't,' he replies.

'I'm not having Rob call the shots from inside the prison,' Carla says.

Kate glances from Carla to her dad, determined to find out what's going on.

'What's Rob got to do with any of this?' she says.

'Let me do this my way,' begs Johnny again. Carla refuses.

'You've had forty odd years to do it your way!'

'Can one of you just tell us what's going on?' Kate demands.

'Carla, please...' begs Johnny.

'Johnny, trust me, this is for your good just as much as mine. But I didn't want to hurt anybody by this, my head's been all over the place.'

Kate's really worried now. 'Carla get to the point!'

'There's no easy way to say this. Last week I found out that Johnny was my dad too which I suppose makes us brother and sisters.'

Aidan is furious and stares hard at Johnny. 'What's she on about?'

'Dad?' asks Kate.

'You'd better start talking!' Aidan yells at his dad. Worse is to come when it turns out that Kate and Aidan's mam died in a car accident after Johnny broke the news to her that he'd had a fling with Carla's mam.

'You've got our mam's blood on your hands! Aidan shouts at Johnny, before thumping his dad.

Over at the Bistro, Carla does her best to ignore Robert and forget their fling at the casino. However, Robert isn't used to being ignored. He tells Carla to think on and warns her he could make life difficult for her. Meanwhile, Nick wants to start planning his and Carla's wedding menu and can't understand why Carla's not keen to sit down with chef Robert to plan it all out.

When the electricity goes off at the Bistro and the staff are sent home, Robert stays on to do some work there alone. Carla finds out he's there on his own so she pops in to see him, to have a quiet word. Unbeknown to them both, Tracy's in the kitchen in her underwear hoping to surprise Robert with a bit of afternoon delight. As Carla and Robert chat at the bar, Tracy overhears everything. She finds out all about Robert sleeping with Carla and it's no longer their secret, not now Tracy knows. Carla and Robert argue at the bar and Carla gives him a brutal summation of his achievements:
'That's why I own a factory … and you own a chef's hat!'

Robert storms out of the Bistro and Carla stays on inside, getting smashed on a bottle of red. In the kitchen out of sight, Tracy hovers in her undies, armed with knowledge of Robert and Carla's infidelity and unsure what to do. As Carla's drinking and Tracy's hovering, Steph's nasty ex-boyfriend Jamie and a pal come into the Bistro.

Jamie's looking to get back at Steph for reporting him to the police over the revenge porn pictures. But Steph's not there, there's only Carla inside. The thugs decide to nick Carla's handbag. Carla's not a woman to be parted from her handbag so she hangs on for dear life, even as Jamie and his pal run with the bag, jump into the car and drive off the cobbles at speed.

Out on the street, Kev and Pat Phelan see what's going on as they come out of the chippy. Phelan jumps in front of the car to try to stop it. Kev pulls him out of the way of the car just in the nick of time. The thugs speed off, Carla's thrown onto the cobbles and she's in a bad way. She's taken to hospital where she's treated for broken bones, internal bleeding and has to have her spleen removed. When she's finally up to seeing visitors, Nick and the Connor clan clutter up her hospital bedside. Roy comes to visit too, en route to stay with his mum Sylvia in Hastings. When it's clear Roy's running late and could miss his train Nick asks Johnny to drive Roy to get his train. Roy demurs but Carla's firm: 'Don't worry, he owes me 40 years of lifts.'

Lying in her hospital bed covered in bruises, Steph goes to visit Carla and tells her about Jamie and his mate, how they were looking for her when they broke into the Bistro, not Carla.
'You're very strong,' she tells Carla.
'It's all smoke and mirrors,' Carla replies.

When Carla is finally released from hospital she's given strong painkillers to help with her pain. She also wears a cast on her broken arm and it's in her favourite colour. Only Carla Connor could make a black cast on a broken arm look so stylish. Although she's in a great deal of pain, Carla agrees to attend a wedding fayre in a posh hotel with Michelle. What she doesn't know is that Tracy and Robert are heading there too. Tracy has a stall advertising her new florist shop, Preston's Petals. Robert books the wedding suite at the hotel, intending to stay overnight with Tracy.

Carla and Michelle also plan to stay there overnight. So, when Tracy finds out that Carla's there, she puts two and two together and gets her sums wrong again. She assumes Carla's after Robert and that's why she's turned up. Jealous Tracy bundles Carla into her hotel room and withholds her painkillers from her, telling her she knows about her afternoon of passion with Robert. Carla doesn't deny it, she's in too much pain to do anything more than give in to whatever Tracy demands. And Tracy makes her demands very clear. She tells Carla she wants her to move out of Weatherfield otherwise she'll tell Nick that Carla cheated on him with Robert. Carla is in so much pain that she can only nod and agree.

Back on the cobbles, Tracy demands that Carla makes a start on moving away. Unwilling to be blackmailed by Tracy, Carla tries to tell Nick the truth, but can't bring herself to let him know that she cheated on him. Instead, she asks Nick if he'll consider selling the Bistro and moving away from the street. He agrees, of course. He loves Carla and is prepared to do anything for her.

When news leaks out that Nick's putting the Bistro up for sale, Tracy encourages Robert to buy it. Nick demands £100,000, but Robert can only raise £90,000 from the bank. Tracy asks Ken if he'll give them the remaining £10,000 they need. Ken refuses Tracy's demand, knowing full well that she can't be trusted.

Determined to get her hands on the Bistro and send Carla packing, Tracy leans on Carla. She tells her to convince Nick to accept Robert's low offer. Carla does her best to confront Tracy. She tells her that Nick will accept Robert's low offer if no higher offers are received. Tracy smirks, so Carla bluffs and says she's doing her a favour by forcing her to get Nick to sell up.
'This is exactly the kick up the tush that I needed to get out of this place,' Carla says.
'Oh! So that's what's happened is it? I've done you a favour?' says Tracy, knowing full well she's got Carla over a barrel.
'Yeah - so thanks, babe,' Carla says.
'No. I'll tell you what's happened, shall I?,' says Tracy. 'You've become my bitch, babe. Always knew you had it in you.'

Carla Connor leaves Coronation Street

Michelle isn't happy when she finds out Carla's thinking of moving away. When she asks Carla where she's planning to go, Carla says the seaside, possibly Devon.
'It'll do your hair no favours, all that sea air,' Michelle notes.
'I'll wear a headscarf then. Like the Queen,' she replies.

Nick and Carla plan their escape and visit Devon where they fall in love with a beautiful cottage. Carla puts her flat up for sale and the first person to view it is none other than Tracy Barlow. Tracy just wants to rub Carla's nose in things, and has no real intention to buy what she calls '…a slapper's boudoir.'   While inside Carla's flat, Tracy reminds her that she has the power to tell Nick about her fling with Robert any time she chooses.

However, once Tracy has left, Nick calls to see Carla, bringing bad news. Their offer on the cottage in Devon has been beaten by another buyer. Carla's distraught, she needs to get away – from Tracy, from Weatherfield, from Underworld, from everyone - as fast as she can. She moves ten thousand pounds from the Underworld account into her own bank. It's money she gives to Tracy so that Robert has the necessary funds to buy the Bistro from Nick. In turn, this gives Nick and Carla the money to buy their dream Devon cottage.

Once the sale of the Bistro goes through, Tracy lords it over the place. She even plans and arranges for a new sign to go up outside – until Robert stops her in her tracks. They argue in the Bistro just as Carla walks in and she gets Tracy's anger thrown at her full force.

But Carla's got more on her mind than Tracy-flaming-Barlow when Nick starts to have problems controlling his moods. It's clear to Nick that the symptoms from his brain injury are returning but he keeps quiet about it, afraid that if Carla finds out he might lose her.

When Carla has a quiet drink with Nick in the Bistro she notices that he's having a soft drink while she's on the red wine. She jokes with him and talk turns to their upcoming wedding.
'Till death us do part,' she says to him.
'In sickness and in health,' he replies quietly.
'Yeah, but we're both as fit as fiddles aren't we?' she smiles, as Nick looks uneasy.
To help control his moods and his rages, Nick goes out running. Carla's surprised when he goes out for a run twice in one day.
'Run like the wind,' she tells him. 'Run to the top of a mountain and pull me down a star.'
'I was thinking of five times around the Red Rec,' he replies.

When his symptoms worsen, Nick visits a consultant and a brain scan is arranged. Trying to cope as best as he can while their wedding plans forge ahead, Nick goes on his stag night in the Rovers and Carla heads into town for her hen party. Along with Carla on the hen night are Maria, Kate, Caz, Beth, Michelle, Cathy, Sally and Gail. Yes, Gail. All the hens are dressed in black and wear long black wigs, trying to out-Carla Carla, and failing. They head to a bar in town, get very, very drunk and when the DJ leaves his booth, Carla takes the mic and the girls start singing *It's Raining Men*. That's when Gail decides she's Carla's best mate after she hosted a pamper party earlier in the week for her daughter-in-law-to-be. And so Gail pushes Kate out of the DJ booth, Kate falls over and the bar staff call the cops. Gail assumes the policemen are strippers when they arrive, and she's all over them shouting "Off! Off!" trying to pull their trousers down. That's when the hens get arrested and taken to the cop shop.

Meanwhile at Nick's stag night in the Rovers, it's a lot more quiet. But it's not a happy gathering as Nick storms out when he starts having trouble with his symptoms again. David follows him out of the pub to the smokers' shelter where Nick tells his brother he feels he has no choice but to call off the wedding to Carla. When Nick and Carla are back at the flat he breaks the news to her that he can't go through with it. Stunned, Carla has trouble taking in the news which has come of the blue.
'Did someone spike my drink?' she asks. 'Am I hallucinating?'

When Nick's rages and moods continue, Carla finally gets him to confess what's going on and goes with him to see the consultant for the results of the scan. The results show that physically Nick's fine but the consultant tells him that he must avoid stress. This prompts Nick to tell Carla that although he might be able to manage going through with the wedding, he doesn't think he can face the stress of moving away. This is news that reaches Tracy who doesn't like the sound of it one little bit. She and Carla have a stand-off in the middle of the Street.

'Move – or I'll blab with a capital B,' Tracy tells Carla. 'You said you were moving away, you daft bint!'
Carla turns on Tracy. 'It's like you're obsessed with me! It would be a compliment... it's like you've almost got a crush! You ruin my life and I won't be responsible for what comes next, ok? And I promise that with a capital P!'

The day of Carla and Nick's wedding dawns and Roy opens the café for a bridal breakfast. Tracy storms in to find out what's going on.
'Good luck today, Carla,' Tracy smirks at the bride-to-be.
'What's luck got to do with it?' Carla replies.

Tracy finds out where Carla's ordered her flowers from, rings up the company and sends Carla's floral bouquets to Crewe instead of Coronation Street. She then pressures Johnny to re-order the wedding flowers from Preston's Petals.

When Johnny finds out what Tracy's done, he locks her inside the Underworld storeroom in an attempt to keep her from ruining his daughter's big day. Tracy kicks and screams inside the storeroom for Johnny to let her free. "I've only got one kidney!" she yells. Johnny does the decent thing and slides Tracy's medication under the storeroom door. And while he's in the factory with Tracy, he's being missed at the wedding. It's Roy who walks Carla up the aisle at the Bistro, with bridesmaids Kate and Michelle following behind.

But as Carla and Nick stand in front of the registrar, Carla whispers to her groom:
'Nick, I need to speak to you. In private. I need to tell you something.'

To everyone's surprise, the ceremony stops. Nick and Carla head to the kitchen at the Bistro for a heart-to-heart where Nick tries to reassure his bride that whatever she has to tell him, he'll be fine with it.
'I know what this is, this is typical Carla,' he says.
'Can't let herself be happy. Can't let someone love her… is always looking for ways to destroy things.'
There's no easy way for Carla to tell Nick what she has to say and so she comes straight out with it. 'I slept with someone. It was a one off, a mistake, I was drunk, but it happened.'
Nick stares at her in shock then demands to know who it was.

'Robert. I'm sorry, so sorry,' Carla says, crying. 'I keep hating myself for this. I need you to forgive me and start again. Please. Nick, when I walked down that aisle and you turned and you looked at me, the way you looked at me, I just thought "Carla you don't deserve this, you don't deserve him".'

Nick is stunned. 'How did I not see it? How?'

'I didn't let you see it. I should have told you straight away and begged your forgiveness -but I beg your forgiveness now. I want to be with you in 50 years time sitting on a rocking chair on some verandah in Devon and I'll turn to you and say "You see, you were right to give me another chance. You were right to believe in us." Please, please, give me that chance Nick.'

Nick is in tears. 'Go,' he tells her. 'Please. Leave me alone and go.'

'I won't give up on us, I can't.' Carla turns to head back to the wedding guests. 'I'm going to go out there and wait for you, Nick. Marry me, please marry me.'

Nick heads to the back yard of the Bistro to clear his head. David joins him and Nick confesses everything that has just happened. David advises his big brother to forgive Carla, telling him that he managed to forgive Kylie after she slept with Nick. This gives Nick plenty to think about. As Nick talks to David outside of the Bistro, inside Roy has a quiet word with Carla.

'Today is not the end of the story, it's a day,' he says. 'Whatever the outcome of this event, tomorrow the story will continue. So do not allow despair to take hold, Carla. Patience is perhaps the most judicious approach right now.'

Carla stands and addresses her wedding guests who are wondering what on earth's going on. 'The wedding is, well, as you might have gathered, off,' she tells them. 'My fault completely. Nick deserves better than me and he, well, he's just… he's gentle and gorgeous and loving…'
Just then Nick comes into the Bistro having made up his mind to forgive and forget.
'Let's get married!' he smiles.

With the ceremony back on, Carla and Nick exchange their vows.
'I, Carla Connor, take you Nicholas Paul Tilsley, to be my lawful wedded husband. To be loving and faithful and loyal for the rest of our lives together.'
'I, Nicholas Paul Tilsley, take you Carla Connor…'
But their vows are interrupted by Tracy who storms into the Bistro. She's been freed from the Underworld storeroom by Aidan after she set the fire alarm off.
'Just rewind!' Tracy demands. 'Have I missed the objections, you know, awful impediments?'
'Lawful impediments!' says Billy.
The registrar tries to carry on. 'If any persons present knows of any lawful impediments to this marriage they should declare it now.'

'Yeah, I do! That slag slept with my boyfriend!' cries
Tracy, pointing at Carla.
'Making a mistake isn't illegal,' says Nick.
Tracy's not happy that her bombshell hasn't
exploded as planned.
'*What*? You *know*?'
'Yeah, sorry to rain on your grenade,' he smiles.
But Tracy's got more grenades to fire down the aisle.
In front of everyone, she reveals that Carla gave her
the money to let Robert buy the Bistro. This is news
that rocks Nick. It makes a mockery of their planned
move to Devon as Nick realises Carla doesn't want to
move because of love but because Tracy was
blackmailing her.
'Is this true?' he asks Carla.
'I gave her the money. It's true... I would have told
you every detail and I will, but there's nothing new
in it, it's all part of the same mistake,' Carla whispers
to Nick. 'We've got our whole futures ahead of us.
Don't let her poison that because no matter what lies
I might have told there's one thing that'll always be
the truth and that is I love you.'
Johnny and Robert bundle Tracy out of the Bistro as
Nick turns to Carla and slips the wedding ring on
her finger.
'I, Nicholas Paul Tilsley, take you, Carla Connor, to
be my lawful wedded wife.'

At the wedding reception for the newly married Mr
and Mrs Tilsley, Nick begins to read his speech. He
tells the guests how happy he was when Carla
proposed to him in the Bistro. And that's when his
face clouds over. He turns to Carla and asks her:

'Was it then? Months ago, was it then? Is that why you proposed?'

'No it wasn't...' she lies.

Nick demands the truth, he needs to know when she slept with Robert and if her proposal was fuelled by guilt.

'Weeks and weeks of lying,' he says. 'Can I ask you a question?'

'I am telling you the truth!' Carla lies again.

'You look me in the eye and it looks the same. Lies and the truth,' he says. He grabs a white linen napkin from the table and thrusts it towards her.

'What colour is this? What colour?'

'Nick, it's white. White.'

'OK. Now tell me it's red. I need to see you lie. Come on Carla, tell me it's red, say it!'

But Carla can't say anything and Nick walks away, leaving Carla Tilsley in tears at the top table.

Johnny has a quiet word with Nick and tries to convince him that Carla really needs him.

'Don't let Tracy win,' he implores Nick.

'It's not Tracy, it's her,' says Nick, pointing at Carla. 'You get upset... you sleep with the chef, you gamble away the factory, you drink yourself into oblivion...'

Nick stops speaking as Gail storms over to her new daughter-in-law and slaps her hard across the face.

'You're not a mother so you don't understand. Hurt my child and I hurt you!' Gail spits at Carla. And then Gail turns to Roy. 'Don't defend her! One day she'll hurt you just like she hurts everyone else.'

'She's right,' Carla says to Roy.

'No, you've a good heart, I've seen it many times, I'll not forget it,' he replies.

Unable to bear staying at the Bistro in the aftermath of the wedding, Carla asks Roy to help get her out. He goes to get his car, but Roy's plan to get back for Carla as quickly as possible comes unstuck when Cathy proposes to him outside of Roy's Rolls. That's when Carla decides to leave of own accord, and gets into her car instead of waiting for Roy. She revs up the engine and when she sees Tracy caught in the car's headlights ahead of her, she aims the car at Tracy and puts her foot to the floor. At the last minute, the car swerves, and Tracy survives, but hits Cathy instead and knocks her unconscious. Carla's erratic driving causes Tyrone to swerve his tow truck to avoid hitting her, and his truck careers into Gail's annex where a dead body is found and buried secrets are unearthed.

The next morning Carla decides she has to get away from Weatherfield, she's caused enough trouble. Through her tears she tells Michelle: 'All the damage I've done, all the guilt in here… it's too much. I could have killed Cathy last night. I really don't see Roy being that forgiving. He is done with me, I know that.'
Before she leaves she goes to the hospital to apologise to Cathy and Roy.
'I know I'm the last person you want to see right now, but I had to come,' she tells Cathy. 'You could have died. I saw Roy's face. I'll never forget it, never.'
'Good,' says Roy. 'If you could think before you lash out, next time.'
'I don't believe I will think, though, do you?' she says. 'I won't forget Roy, I'll keep on trying.'

Roy's anger and hurt is palatable. All he can manage to say is: 'Tomorrow is another day... and so on.' Carla leaves the hospital and Cathy persuades Roy to return to Coronation Street to say a proper farewell to his friend.

On the street, Carla says her tearful goodbyes to Kate, Aidan and Michelle. Nick appears after he's been for a run. Carla raises a hand and gives a tentative wave, but he ignores her, too hurt to speak. She hugs Johnny.

'I love you dad. Come on, gotta go.'

But just before she gets into Johnny's Jaguar, she spots Tracy outside of Preston's Petals.

'Open goal, Barlow. Hit me,' she says but Tracy stays quiet. 'Got no fight left?'

Tracy nods towards the car. 'Well you're the one with the engine running.'

'All these years of hating me...' says Carla.

'Loathing, get it right,' Tracy replies.

'... it suddenly struck me. Did you really want to be me? Because it's not all it's cracked up to be.'

Tracey nods towards Johnny waiting by his car. 'Well at least you get a send off, eh?'

'Yeah, I get a send off. I just didn't get a husband or a kid.'

'It's a bit too late for your life story. Well, go on then, go. Go and cry on somebody else's shoulder.'

'We're done,' says Carla and walks away from the woman who has made her life hell.

Just then the Weatherfield Wayfarer arrives.

'What's this clown doing?' asks Johnny when he spies Roy at the front of the bus.

Roy and Carla share a few final words.

'You're cutting it fine,' she tells him, in tears. 'So you didn't think I was worth the taxi fare?'

'You are who you are,' Roy says. 'Don't lose that. Perhaps you could learn to love yourself as much as we all love you. Fresh start, calmer waters.'

'Come and paddle,' Carla tells him through her tears. 'Do it.'

She puts her hands to Roy's face and kisses him, in tears.

'I will,' says Roy.

Carla gets into the passenger seat of her dad's car and as he drives her off the cobbles she turns to wave to Roy.

Will Carla ever return to Coronation Street?
Ah, now there's a question!

SOURCES

Online

ITV Coronation Street website:
http://www.itv.com/corrie

ITV Coronation Street YouTube channel
https://www.youtube.com/coronationstreet

Corrie.net - Coronation Street fan website
http://www.corrie.net

Coronation Street Blog
http://coronationstreetupdates.blogspot.com

Corriepedia
http://coronationstreet.wikia.com/wiki/Corriepedia

DVD

Coronation Street 2000-2009, Network 2011

ACKNOWLEDGEMENTS

The author wishes to thank:

Barry Smith

The team at the Coronation Street Blog

Corriepedia

Coronation Street fans on Twitter, especially @AliKingFan4 and @RachieAliette

Cover artwork by illustrator Jo Blakeley

Website - pickledjo.dunked.com
Twitter - twitter.com/pickledjo
Facebook - www.facebook.com/Pickledjo

ABOUT THE AUTHOR

Glenda Young is a writer and author of the following books:

Deirdre: A Life on Coronation Street. Century / Random House / ITV Publishing (2015)

A Perfect Duet. The diary of Roy and Hayley Cropper. An unofficial Coronation Street companion book. FBS Publishing e-book and paperback (2014)

Norman Bates with a Briefcase. The Richard Hillman Story. An unofficial Coronation Street companion book. KDP e-book (2014) and CreateSpace paperback (2016)

Coronation Street: The Complete Saga. Updated from 2008-2010 (ITV / Carlton Publishing 2010)

Coronation Street: The Novel. Updated from 2003-2008 (ITV / Carlton Publishing 2008)

Editor of Coronation Street fan websites:

Coronation Street Blog
http://coronationstreetupdates.blogspot.com

Corrie.net
http://www.corrie.net

Find out more at glendayoungbooks.com

Printed in Poland
by Amazon Fulfillment
Poland Sp. z o.o., Wrocław

64410263R00070